ON COMPROMISE

AND ROTTEN COMPROMISES

ON COMPROMISE
AND ROTTEN COMPROMISES

❦

AVISHAI MARGALIT

PRINCETON UNIVERSITY PRESS

PRINCETON AND OXFORD

Copyright © 2010 by Princeton University Press
Published by Princeton University Press, 41 William Street,
Princeton, New Jersey 08540

In the United Kingdom: Princeton University Press, 6 Oxford Street,
Woodstock, Oxfordshire OX20 1TW

Library of Congress Cataloging-in-Publication Data

Margalit, Avishai, 1939–
On compromise and rotten compromises / Avishai Margalit.
p. cm.
Includes bibliographical references (p.   ) and index.
ISBN 978-0-691-13317-1 (hardcover : alk. paper) 1. Compromise (Ethics)
2. Political science—Philosophy. I. Title.
BJ1431.M28   2009
170—dc22
2009011807

British Library Cataloging-in-Publication Data is available

This book has been composed in Minion typeface

Printed on acid-free paper. ∞

press.princeton.edu

Printed in the United States of America

1 3 5 7 9 10 8 6 4 2

In memory of my parents,
Miriam and Moshe

CONTENTS

❧

ACKNOWLEDGMENTS

❧

I DELIVERED TWO Tanner lectures at Stanford University in 2005. The themes of these lectures are the basis of chapters 1 and 3. The lectures were closely scrutinized by four exceptionally powerful commentators from varied fields of learning: John Ferjohn, Lee Ross, Samuel Scheffler, and Tamar Schapiro. I was also very lucky to receive highly searching comments from Kenneth Arrow, Moshe Halbertal, and Amelie Rorty, who read the Tanner lectures and wrote detailed comments. Edna Ullmann-Margalit read the entire manuscript, and her contribution, as always, is invaluable.

I thank Mike Borns, Julia Bernheim, and Lauren Lepow for helping me at various stages in matters of language and style.

I am to be blamed for the shortcomings of the book, but without the help I received, there would have been many more.

ON COMPROMISE

AND ROTTEN COMPROMISES

INTRODUCTION
WHY COMPROMISE?

The Concern

ALBERT EINSTEIN is credited with the warning "Beware of rotten compromises."[1] My book is an effort to explain and support this warning.

But the book is about much more. It is about peace and compromise.

More specially: what compromises we are not allowed to make for the sake of peace.

The short answer is: rotten compromises are not allowed, even for the sake of peace. Other compromises should be dealt with on a retail basis, one by one: they should be judged on their merit. Only rotten compromises should be ruled out on a wholesale basis. Even though the book is about compromises that we should avoid, come what may, its main goal is to leave the widest (morally) possible room for compromises made for the sake of peace, including cases in which peace is achieved at the expense of justice. The book is in pursuit of just *a* peace, rather than of a *just* peace. Peace can be justified without being just.

This is not an easy claim to make, but this is the claim I am making.

The compromises discussed in the book are political compromises, rather than personal ones. The distinction is not always clear. Some personal deals have immense political implications. Robert Oppenheimer's role in creating the atomic bomb is often referred to as a Faustian bargain. According to Freeman Dyson, the deal was this: an atomic bomb in exchange for the chance to do physics on a grand scale,[2] or, more to the point, Oppenheimer's being in charge of doing physics on a grand scale. Whatever the real details of Oppenheimer's Faustian pact are, the political implication of the atomic bomb is as obvious as its mushroom cloud.

I see a rotten political compromise as an agreement to establish or maintain an inhuman regime, a regime of cruelty and humiliation, that is, a regime that does not treat humans as humans. Throughout the book I use "inhuman" to denote extreme manifestations of not treating humans as humans. Inhuman in the sense of cruel, savage, and barbarous behavior conveys only one element of "inhuman" as I use the word; humiliation is another element. Humiliation, as I see it, is already not treating humans as humans, but humiliation intensified by cruelty equals "inhuman." So a fusion of cruelty and humiliation is what an inhuman regime consists of.

The idea of an inhuman regime, a regime of cruelty and humiliation, guides my understanding of rotten compromises. The basic claim is that we should beware of agreeing, even passively, to establish or maintain a regime of cruelty and humiliation—in short, an inhuman regime.

Many bad things popped out of Pandora's box, and choosing inhuman regimes as the bad thing to avoid at all costs calls for justification.

Inhuman regimes erode the foundation of morality. Morality rests on treating humans as humans; not treating humans as humans undermines the basic assumption of morality. I draw a distinction between *morality* and *ethics*. Morality is about how human relations should be in virtue of our being human and in virtue of nothing else.

Ethics, in contrast, is about what relations we *should* have with other people in virtue of some special relationships we *have* with them, such as family relations or friendship.

Morality, by its very nature, is based on the category of belonging to humanity, in the sense of belonging to the human species. The assault on humanity inflicted when humans are treated as nonhumans undermines the very project of morality, the project of constituting human relations as they should be.

For the sake of defending morality we end up with a stern injunction: rotten compromise must be avoided, come what may. But what does the "come what may" come to? Chapters 4 and 5 are meant to answer this question. The upshot is that the "come what may" should be taken quite literally.

Let me stress again, the book contains stern warnings against rotten compromises, yet its aim is to provide strong advocacy for compromises in general, and compromises for the sake of peace in particular. It limits wholesale prohibitions on compromises to the bare minimum. Limiting wholesale prohibitions to the bare minimum does not mean that all compromises are justified. There might be good reasons to reject a particular compromise on the ground that it is unfair, unreasonable, or untimely. Selling Manhattan (in 1624) for merchandise worth 60 guilders was not a terribly good idea for the Native Americans involved, nor, for that matter, was the selling of Alaska by the Russians (in 1867) for 7.2 million dollars.

I do not subscribe to the adage "A lean compromise is better than a fat lawsuit."[3] But I do claim that only rotten compromises should be prohibited in all circumstances. Other compromises should be evaluated on their merit, case by case. Some may turn out to be shady deals (deals with suspicious motives), shoddy deals (exchange of phony goods, "beads and buttons," for true valuables), or shabby deals (exploitative ones, taking advantage of the vulnerability of the weak party). These are all forms of morally bad deals, yet given the alternatives, they might on occasion be justified. Rotten compromises are different. They are never *justified*; at best, they may be *excused*.

Rotten compromises usually are at the heart of darkness. Extreme forms of racist regimes are the epitome of not treating humans as humans, and constitute a direct affront to the assumption of shared humanity. A compromise to establish or maintain racist regimes is the epitome of rottenness.

Indeed, one depressing example of a rotten agreement has the characteristics of Joseph Conrad's celebrated *Heart of Darkness*.[4] Though this example is a clear case of a rotten compromise, it blurs the line between a personal rotten deal and a collective rotten deal. It concerns the private domain of King Leopold II of Belgium over the Congo, under the sham of "enlightening Africa." If there have ever been regimes of cruelty and humiliation, this king's personal rule of that colony, between 1880 and 1908, is surely among them. The population of the Congo was not only enslaved and inhumanely brutalized, but also half of it (between eight and ten million) was slaughtered in order to "lighten the darkness of Africa."[5] Thus Conrad's book, as we learn from Adam Hochschild's *King Leopold's Ghost*, is not an allegory but a reality. Leopold's Congo Free State constituted a direct assault on the very notion of shared humanity.[6]

Two types of agreements were involved in the workings of the Congo Free State. One dealt with the acquisition of land in the Congo, usually from local chieftains. Agreements of this type can hardly be described as compromises. They were extracted by threats and direct intimidation. The other type of agreements, such as those concluded among

Leopold II, France, and the United States (1884–1885), are compromises—and very rotten ones at that. They contain trade advantages in the Congo in exchange for the recognition of Leopold's inhuman regime. These rotten compromises differ from shady, shoddy, and shabby compromises; they are morally wrong at all times. Leopold II ran the Congo as his private realm. One may therefore say that agreements with Leopold, bad as they were, were personal agreements, not political compromises between two collectives. This is technically true, but only technically.

Compromise, an Ambivalent Concept

The concept of compromise, I believe, should take center stage in micromorality (dealing with individuals' interactions) as well as in macromorality (dealing with political units). After all, we very rarely attain what is first on our list of priorities, either as individuals or as collectives. We are forced by circumstances to settle for much less than what we aspire to. We compromise. We should, I believe, be judged by our compromises more than by our ideals and norms. Ideals may tell us something important about what we would like to be. But compromises tell us who we are.[7]

The compromises we eventually settle on, if we are lucky, are our second-best choices, and often not even that. But, again, they tell us more about our moral standing than does an account of our first priority.[8]

Yet the concept of compromise is neither at center stage in philosophical discussion nor even on its back burner. One reason why compromise does not occur as a philosophical topic stems from the philosophical bias in favor of ideal theory. Compromise looks messy, the dreary stuff of day-to-day politics. It looks very different from the ideal theory of micro- or macromorality. Indeed ideal theory concerns norms and ideals, not second bests. But removing compromise from moral theory is like removing friction from physics, claiming that it belongs to engineering.

Compromise is an ambivalent concept. It carries opposing evaluative forces. It is a "boo-hurrah" concept—a positive notion signaling human cooperation, coupled with a negative notion signaling betrayal of high-minded principles. Compromise is regarded on some occasions as an expression of goodwill, and on other occasions as being wishy-washy.

An *ambivalent* concept is different from an *essentially contested* concept.[9] The latter has an uncontested and uncontestable good connotation, and the contest deals only with what represents the best example of its kind. During the Cold War "democracy" was an essentially contested term between communists and liberals. For communists, the People's Democracy of Eastern Europe was a "real" democracy, and liberal democracy was a mere "formal" democracy; whereas for liberals it was the liberal democracy of Western Europe that was real, and the People's Democracy a euphemism for oppressive party dictatorship. The point here, however, is that both sides regarded "democracy" as a good word, each trying to appropriate its positive connotation for its own ideology. Ambivalent words are different; they are both good and bad.

But then we should remember that politics is not an exercise in linguistic philosophy, and that a contest about the use of words is never about words alone. What is contested in the case of "compromise" is the very idea of compromise: is it good—like friendship and peace—or is it bad, like timidity and spinelessness?

Superficially, it sounds silly to ask whether compromises are good or bad, much like asking whether bacteria are good or bad: we cannot live without bacteria, though sometimes we die because of bacteria. Yet that asymmetry makes the question about the goodness and the badness of bacteria, as well as those of compromise, worth asking. We have ten times as many bacteria in our bodies as we have cells, and many of those are vital for our existence. A small number of bacteria are pathogenic and cause disease, and with the proper treatment, we may get rid of them. Similarly, compromises are vital for social life, even though some compromises are pathogenic. We need antibiotics to resist pathogenic bacteria, and we need to actively resist rotten compromises that are lethal for the moral life of a body politic.

Tension between Peace and Justice

I believe that beyond the ambivalence toward compromise and the spirit of compromise lurks a deep tension between peace and justice. Peace and justice may even demand two incompatible temperaments, one of compromise for the sake of peace, and the other of a Michael Kohlhaas–like bloody-mindedness, to let justice prevail, come what may.[10] In the Hebrew Bible peace and justice live in harmony: "justice and peace kissed" (Psalm 85:11). By contrast, for dark Heraclitus, peace and justice live in disharmony: "Justice is strife."[11] The Talmud recognizes the tension between the two: "When there is strict justice there is no peace and where there is peace there is no strict justice."[12] The spirit of peace, for the Talmudists, is the spirit of compromise as manifested in arbitration; the spirit of justice— "Let justice pierce the mountain"[13]—is manifested in trial.[14]

Moses, in the eyes of the rabbis, incarnates the spirit of justice, and his brother Aaron incarnates the spirit of compromise and peace. Moses is admired. Aaron is loved.

The tension between peace and justice is at the center of this book; compromise is the go-between. I am particularly interested in the moral status of compromise made for the sake of peace at the expense of justice. How far can we go for peace by giving up on justice? Quite a distance, I say, but not the whole way. This is the short answer. My long answer is this whole book.

Declaring that two terms are in tension is often a way of muddying the waters and declaring them deep: tension between peace and justice needs elucidation. We tend to view peace and justice as *complementary* goods, like fish and chips, whereas in actuality peace and justice stand to each other as *competing* goods, like tea and coffee. The tension is due to the possibility of a trade-off between peace and justice: to gain peace, we may be forced to pay in justice.

Levi Eshkol, a former prime minster of Israel and a hero of mine, had the reputation of being a relentless compromiser; a tall story had it that when asked whether he would like tea or coffee, he answered, "Half and half," the idea being that the spirit of compromise may blind one to the fact of competing goods among which one has to choose. The trade-off between peace and justice is no laughing matter; it can be tragic, and the sense of this tragic choice pervades the book.

Not everyone agrees that peace and justice may collide. One objection to that view is the idea that peace is a constitutive part of justice and hence an essential component of justice: more peace is more justice. A different, yet related, view is that peace is only casually linked to justice: more peace may bring about more justice.[15]

This is not my view. An analogy may explain my position. Caffeine was regarded as essential to coffee, or at least as a contributing factor to coffee's main characteristic, that of be-

ing a stimulant. Removing caffeine from coffee was once in-
conceivable. But we can remove caffeine from coffee beans,
thus creating a drink that competes with coffee: decaffeinated coffee. Peace is the caffeine of justice: it enhances justice.
But peace, like decaffeinated coffee, can compete with justice.
Between peace and justice there may exist a trade-off, much
as between coffee and decaffeinated coffee. It is because of
those situations of trade-off between peace and justice that I
talk about tension between them.

Vacillating between Lasting Peace and Just Peace

Political philosophers have dealt with the notion of a lasting
("permanent") peace, but hardly ever with the notion of a just
peace. This is so, perhaps, because philosophers feel that the
idea of a just peace may be the enemy of the notion of just
(i.e., simply) a peace, in the cliché sense according to which
the best is the enemy of the good. It is preferable, in this view,
to worry about the stability of peace than to worry about
whether or not it is just. Another reason is, perhaps, that since
both peace and peacemaking seem so good and just in and of
themselves, there is no need for justification. But this explanation won't do. After all, most philosophers are not pacifists
who believe that peace is justified at any price. Many thinkers
maintain that there are just wars, which should be preferred
to extremely unjust states of peace. To be sure, there is a difference between *just* peace and *justifiable* peace; not every injustice justifies going to war. Still, most thinkers would agree,
some states of injustice justify war. Yet while there are many
intensive debates about just and unjust wars, there are no parallel and independent debates about just and unjust peace.

Concern with Cruel Humiliation

The issue of cruel humiliation as a major moral concern looms large in my book *The Decent Society*. This time, I address extreme forms of humiliation, namely, humiliation combined with cruelty. I am concerned about humiliation as a loss of human dignity, rather than about social or national honor. But the sense of national humiliation plays an important political role in the effort to achieve compromise in the form of a peace agreement.

It seems that the orthopedic task of a peace treaty—to stiffen up the nation's posture—is almost impossible to achieve. A peace agreement by nature requires painful compromises, and there will always be those for whom any compromise is seen as shameful capitulation, those for whom dying "sword in hand" is preferable to accepting any compromise. But this in itself—the fact that some will always regard a peace treaty as capitulation—should not *morally* weigh heavily with the peacemakers. There is, however, a related consideration, the *moral* consideration of honor and humiliation, that any peace treaty should take into account.

The Munich Syndrome

It was Isaiah Berlin who initiated me into the topic of compromise and rotten compromise by conveying to me a strong sense of the importance of the spirit of compromise in politics, but also by conveying the formative experience of his generation: the Munich agreement as a definitive rotten compromise.

The appeasement trauma never left Berlin and his generation. For a few days during the Suez campaign of 1956, Eden's obsession with appeasement resonated with Berlin, as did his idea that if Nasser were not stopped, he might become un-stoppable—only until he realized that the analogy between the real Hitler and the Mussolini-on-the-Nile was an analogy gone wild.

We were discussing the Suez affair and I complained in-dignantly of the misuse of the Munich agreement by para-noid politicians: those who see Chamberlain's umbrella, the symbol of defeatism, everywhere.

Berlin admitted as much and added a story. A man was seen banging fiercely on top of a whistling boiling kettle. "What are you doing?" the man was asked. "I can't stand steam locomotives." "But this is a kettle, not a locomotive." "Yes, yes, I know, but you have to kill them when they are still young."

I suspect that the often-used analogy of appeasing Nasser as Mussolini-on-the-Nile, or Saddam as Hitler-on-the-Tigris, is of the kettle-as-young-locomotive kind.

As much as I want to use the Munich agreement as the paradigm case for a rotten compromise, I am acutely aware of its obnoxious role in political propaganda.

As for Berlin, what may have kept his appeasement trauma at bay was a deeply held belief (which he shared with his mentor, the historian H.A.L. Fisher) that history is "one damn thing after another." Hence there is no room for read-ing history as a series of prefigurations, with one figure—say, Hitler—heralding another figure in the future, and every compromise covered by Chamberlain's umbrella. The issue of compromise was for Berlin the flip side of the golden coin of moral courage and integrity. His personal fear was that his tendency to seek compromise was a sign of timidity. Yet he set as high a premium on compromise as did Edmund Burke in his celebrated speech of March 22, 1775, on the question of conciliation with America: "All government—indeed every human benefit and enjoyment, every virtue and every prudent act—is founded on compromise and barter."[16] By barter, I presume, Burke meant give-and-take. For Burke, too, compromise is not just a matter of politics but one of personal strategy. But then it seems that compromise is one of those values both necessary and impossible. Moreover, it is necessary and impossible precisely when it matters most— namely, when, for the sake of peace, we have to compromise justice.

This leads me to a related lifelong concern of Isaiah Berlin that made a deep impression on me: his famous insistence that values may conflict with one another and cannot be reduced to one another. Berlin rejoiced in the clash of values as an expression of human variety, even when he saw the tragic side of such clashes. I can almost hear him say, with Walt Whitman–like exuberance, "In holding the values we do, we do contradict ourselves. Very well then, we contradict ourselves. But then we are large and contain multitudes."

The clash, or the apparent clash, at the center of political thought is that between freedom and equality. I believe the clash that should bother us most is that between peace and justice.

The Concern with the Passive Side

A typical rotten compromise has two sides: one is the perpetrator of a regime of cruelty and humiliation, and the other is a passive participant, merely lending its support to such a regime by signing the agreement. I am concerned with the perspective of the passive side. With the evil perpetrator, the rotten compromise is the least of the evil things it does.

Its rottenness lies in actually establishing and maintaining an inhuman regime, a regime of systematic cruelty and humiliation. But the rottenness of the passive side is in lending support to the active side. It is the British passive side in the Munich agreement that interests me, not the Nazi active side. The Nazi regime is rotten not so much for the agreement it signed, as for creating the reality that made the treaty rotten.

In the case in which both sides to the agreement are perpetrators of cruelty and humiliation—as, for example, in the case of the Molotov-Ribbentrop pact of August 23, 1939, also known as the Hitler-Stalin pact—the issue is not the rottenness of the pact itself but of their very cruel deeds.

The Choice between Stalin and Hitler

One large issue still remains to be covered: what about a passive side (say, Churchill) having an agreement with one perpetrator (Stalin) against another (Hitler)? Is such an agreement rotten? This is a rather misleading presentation of the choice, since Germany invaded Russia. It was not, simply, a choice out of compromise of siding with one perpetrator against the other. But still the issue of choosing between the two stood before Churchill.

The choice was not an issue of the lesser evil, but a choice between radical evil and evil, Hitler being the radical evil. In any case, I felt the need to deal with morally comparing Stalinism and Hitlerism.

Personally I find this particular comparison painful to carry out. I am keenly aware that the heroism and the sacrifice of the Red Army and of the Soviet civilians, more than anything else, brought about the defeat of Nazi Germany. Moreover, as a Jew, I am intensely conscious that many Jews were rescued by the Red Army, regardless of the still-open question whether the Soviets made a special effort to rescue Jews during the evacuation of 1941. The claim of a special decree by the Kremlin to give priority to the evacuation of the Jewish population during the rapid advancement of the German army may be nothing more than a propaganda myth. But it is not a myth that many Jews, with or without priority, were saved, thanks to the Soviets, among them, devastatingly, only a very few members of my large extended family. Like many others, I feel an immense gratitude toward Soviet Russia for its role in saving the world from Hitler. I believe that the effort to belittle the Soviets' role in the defeat of Germany is despicable. Yet, in the context of prewar Europe, the moral question for someone like Churchill of whether to side with Stalin or with Hitler, both ruling over cruel and humiliating regimes, should be addressed. Indeed, I undertake a moral comparison of the two in the book's conclusion.

The moral significance of the Second World War is a topic I endlessly discussed with Stuart Hampshire. The war was his formative experience, and he convinced me that it should also be at the center of my generation's thinking. Hampshire had perfect pitch for moral ambiguities. I tried, perhaps by osmosis, to learn from him not just the sense of the twentieth century but also its sensibility.

If the book enunciates a firm admonition against making rotten compromises, it also sends a word of warning against a bloody-minded uncompromising cast of mind—the mind of the sectarian. I received a stiff warning of that kind myself from no less a figure than Irving Howe. It made a lasting impression on me. Here is the story of my first meeting with Howe, which ended with a warning.

In the gloomy days following the 1973 Yom Kippur War, a delegation of intellectuals from the United States came to

Jerusalem and stayed at the illustrious King David Hotel. There were no visitors in Israel at the time, and these were perhaps the first to arrive after the war and just before the elections. I was on the slate of a tiny peace party on the left called *Moked*. We knew almost all our voters by name. The quality of the support was never in doubt—it was the party of the intelligentsia—but the numbers were very much in question.

In the event, we got a single seat in the Knesset out of 120. The party advocated a two-state solution, Israel and Palestine. During those Golda Meir days, the mere mention of a Palestinian state was a heresy that guaranteed for its adherents a place in the frozen lake of Dante's ninth circle of hell. The frozen lake has melted since then. The idea of two states has now become an Israeli consensus, one that many Israelis express in public, but that not enough Israelis believe in private.

Ariel Sharon, the commander of my unit in that war, was at the time the great unifier of the Right. He forced Begin's party and the General Zionist Party to form an election bloc—the bloc that later succeeded in bringing Begin to power. Against army regulations, Sharon started campaigning for this bloc while still in uniform. Worried that Sharon would set about stirring things up in the army, the government ordered that anyone listed on a party's slate be immediately released from service duty for the duration of the election campaign. So, along with Sharon, I found myself released from active service, and headed from the Suez Canal back to Israel proper.

On the day I arrived home in Jerusalem, I was assigned to meet that delegation from the United States at the King David Hotel, to present to them the ideas of our *Moked* party, as other parties were presenting their own ideas. I was relatively young and very angry, so I guess I gave the speech of an angry young man, believing then, as I still do now, that it was Golda

Meir's government that had brought upon us that horrendous war. When it was all over, two people approached me: "My name is Irving Howe." "My name is Michael Walzer." As both names rang a huge bell, I was surprised and impressed. Then Howe said to me, "I agree with a great deal of what you said. But why do you promote a party that has no chance of winning elections? Why don't you join the Labor Party and change it from within? They will surely let you people be active among them. Sharon is doing politics; you are not." Then came the punch line. "Let me tell you. From my experience, the one thing you should avoid at all costs is becoming a sect. Sectarian politics is a terrible waste. I feel that you are in danger of becoming sectarian, as I was in my youth." I sensed that Irving Howe had said something disturbingly important. In all the years since, I have been haunted by Irving's commandment: Thou shall not be sectarian. Sectarian politics is the opposition to the spirit of compromise.

Chapter 6 is an effort to describe the cast of mind Howe warned me against.

So here is the telegraphic message of the book: On the whole, political compromises are a good thing. Political compromises for the sake of peace are a very good thing. Shabby, shady, and shoddy compromises are bad but not sufficiently bad to be always avoided at all costs, especially not when they are concluded for the sake of peace. Only rotten compromises are bad enough to be avoided at all costs. But then, rotten compromises are a mere tiny subset of the large set of possible political compromises.

I tried to shape the book in discursive lecturing style, informal, anecdotal, autobiographical, only lightly footnoted, with a direct appeal to the listener, as "you" rather than an indirect formal appeal to "the reader." The danger of this lecture style

is in tilting the balance between the rhetorical and the logical in favor of the rhetorical. In philosophy, this is a serious
danger. When it comes to ethics, the rhetorical may turn into
sermonizing, the danger being not in disregarding the truth,
but in disregarding arguments and distinctions. I try to argue
by making distinctions, hoping to keep away from sermonizing as much as I can.

Whether I succeeded is for you to judge.

- 1 -

Two Pictures of Political Compromise

Appeasement

ON SEPTEMBER 29, 1938, Hitler, Chamberlain, Daladier, and Mussolini met in Munich and reached an agreement to transfer from Czechoslovakia to Germany the Sudetenland, a narrow strip of land populated by ethnic Germans. In return, Hitler promised not to make any further territorial demands on Europe. In March 1939, the German army seized all of Czechoslovakia; the rest is history, horrendous history.

The Munich agreement became the symbol of a rotten compromise, a compromise one should not sign under any circumstances. "Appeasement" became the label for the policy that led to the Munich agreement. Since the agreement was perceived as rotten, the term "appeasement" went through a total readjustment: it lost its positive sense of bringing calm and peace and came to mean surrendering to the demands of a bully just because he is a bully. "Appeaser" became a term synonymous with "delusional person"—one who feeds a crocodile, hoping it will eat him last, a saying attributed to Churchill.

Is the Munich agreement in fact a clear case of a rotten compromise? Was the Munich agreement the outcome of a compromise? A preliminary effort to answer these two questions will give us a handle on the general concern of my book, namely, what is the distinction between a compromise and a rotten compromise, a compromise one should not accept under any circumstances?

For an agreement to be a compromise, the parties to the agreement should make mutual concessions. One of the criticisms of the Munich agreement is that Hitler made no concessions on his part, aside, perhaps, from vague promises to refrain from further territorial demands on Europe. Another criticism is that the agreement was nothing but an act of coercion by Germany, and coercion is no compromise.

Churchill, later to be lionized, roared against the agreement by raising these two lines of criticism. In his House of Commons speech (October 5, 1938) he used the following analogy: "One pound was demanded at pistol's point. When it was given, two pounds were demanded at pistol's point. Finally, the dictator consented to take one pound, seventeen shillings and six pence, and the rest in promises of good will for the future."[1] In my opinion, the proverbial "pistol's point" refers to coercion rather than to compromise; the retreat in demand from two pounds to £1 17s 6d tells us that Hitler's insignificant concession amounts to no concession at all. So the Munich agreement, as Churchill understood it, was not a compromise but a total surrender: Hitler bullied Chamberlain and Chamberlain capitulated.

There is no question that the Munich agreement involved coercion. But that coercion was exerted on Czechoslovakia— a victim of the agreement, not a party to it. As for Britain and France, it is more accurate to describe them as compromising at the expense of Czechoslovakia than to see them as giving in to a direct coercive threat.[2]

The relation between compromise and coercion, as we shall see, is pretty convoluted. But one thing is clear-cut: the closer it is to a case of compromise, the further it is from co-ercion. Yet it is conceptually possible for an agreement to be a clear case of rotten compromise, and not a clear case of compromise, much as a clear case of a lapsed Catholic is not a clear case of a Catholic. Nevertheless, a rotten compromise *is* a compromise, unlike a rotten stone that is powder and not stone.[3]

The question of whether the Munich agreement is a compromise is linked to, though not determined by, the question of whether the Munich agreement was coercive toward Britain or France. Coercion, unlike compulsion, involves threats. In the absence of threat, there is no coercion. To evaluate coercion, I maintain, we should adopt the subjective view-point of the one presumably threatened. The justification for accepting the subjective viewpoint is that coercion, unlike compulsion, hinges on a communicative act of threaten-ing. The victim should understand the act of threatening as having a coercive effect, and the way the prospective victim understands the situation is crucial.

As far as Britain is concerned, those who signed the Munich agreement did not perceive it as yielding to a coercive threat, but as a genuine compromise. As far as I know, Chamberlain never claimed that he was coerced to sign the agreement, and there is no reason to suppose that he defended his stand in bad faith. The Munich agreement, according to the subjec-tive test, is a compromise. But is it a rotten compromise?

The Munich agreement is a rotten compromise, not pre-dominantly because of its contents, but because it was Hitler who signed it. Imagine that instead of the dreadful Hitler, it was the dignified Walther Rathenau who made demands on Sudetenland. Imagine that he made those demands on behalf of the Weimar Republic, in the name of the Sudeten Germans' right to self-determination, arguing that Czechoslovakia, true to its name, meant to serve only two peoples—seven million Czechs and two million Slovaks—showing a complete disregard for the three million Sudeten Germans' forced inclusion in Czechoslovakia. Even if we believe that argument to be flawed—for it means, among other things, that Czechoslovakia had to give up its natural and man-made defenses against Germany—it is still a moral argument and by no means a rotten one.

So if the content of the agreement is not shamefully rotten, what is? It cannot be the motive for signing the agreement that makes it rotten. There was nothing shameful in Chamberlain's yearning for peace as a motive for signing the agreement. Even Churchill, not a great fan of Chamberlain, recognized his sincerity: "No one has been a more resolute and uncompromising struggler for peace than the Prime Minister."[4] So the purity of Chamberlain's peace-seeking motive was never in dispute.

The agreement cannot be rotten just because it was based on an error in political judgment—putting Britain's trust in the hands of a serial betrayer—for that is an empirical blunder, not a moral sin. So what is rotten in the Munich pact? My answer is that the one with whom it was signed, and not what was signed, makes it rotten. A pact with Hitler was a pact with radical evil, evil as an assault on morality itself. Not recognizing Hitler as radically evil was a moral failure on top of a bad error of political judgment.

True, Hitler in 1938 was not the Hitler of the war years. But what Nazism stood for should have already been clear in the thirties: it stood for radical evil. By that, I mean not just committing evil but trying to eradicate the very idea of morality—by actively rejecting the premise on which morality is predicated, namely, our shared humanity. Virulent global Nazi racism was a total effort to eliminate the sense of shared humanity, so to compromise with Hitler was to compromise with someone who undermined morality itself. It was right, morally right, for the Allies to declare an all-out war on Germany, and to proclaim any effort to come to terms with Nazi Germany as basically rotten.

Not every agreement with Hitler's regime is rotten by definition. For example, had the deal offered to the Allies by Adolf Eichmann on behalf of the SS's highest authorities been accepted, bartering for the lives of a million Hungarian Jews by supplying Nazi Germany with ten thousand trucks for civilian use, I would not have considered its acceptance by the Allies rotten. Such a deal would have saved human beings from humiliation and death under Hitler's regime. (I shall return to the "Blood for Trucks" deal in chapter 4.)

My Concerns

I started with the example of Munich to pave the way for my two concerns: compromise and peace. A moral distinction must be drawn between compromise and rotten compromise—a compromise one should avoid under any circumstances. It is, I believe, a fitting distinction. It should help us sort out the relation between peace and justice.

As I mentioned in the introduction when I presented my interest in justified peace, I am interested first and foremost in political compromise: compromise between groups and states rather than compromise between individuals. Rotten individual compromises, personal "pacts with the devil," concern me here only as they pertain to individuals who negotiate for a collective—say, Neville Chamberlain in Munich, or the "great compromiser" Roger Sherman of Connecticut, rather than Dr. Faustus in his personal pact with the devil. In fact, individuals are going to play central roles in my court of history. I shall present individuals making compromises that strongly reflect on them personally, but in these cases the compromise under review will be a political compromise, on behalf of a collective.

In what follows I use from time to time examples of personal pacts, but I use them as useful analogies to political pacts, and not as a subject that stands on its own.

Two Pictures

The idea of political compromise is caught between two pictures of politics: politics as economics and politics as religion. Roughly speaking, in the economic picture of politics everything is subject to compromise. Compromise is not always desirable or prudent, but it is always possible. In the religious picture, there are things over which we must never compromise.

The religious picture is in the grip of the idea of the holy. The holy is not negotiable, let alone subject to compromise. Crudely put, one cannot compromise over the holy without compromising the holy. Conversely, in the economic picture of politics, compromise is at the heart of politics, and the ability to compromise is highly praised. That politics is the art of compromise is a tired cliché. Economic life is based on the idea of substitution: one good can be replaced by another, and this enables exchanges in the market. Exchanges leave room for negotiation, and where there is room for negotiation, there is room for compromise. Compromise has an internal relation to what is exchangeable and divisible.

Economic products serving as the model for politics make it seem as if compromise is always possible. Not so with re-

ligion. However, religions, by which I mean religious institutions and religious states, make political compromises all
the time; they routinely develop elaborate justifications and
techniques to carry out their compromises. The politics of
the holy leaves plenty of room for compromise in matters
profane. It may in practice even be engaged in compromise
in matters holy, but the logic of the holy as an ideal type is the
negation of the idea of compromise.

Modern politics is seized by these two irreconcilable pictures. There is, of course, nothing surprising about secular
modern states' being subject to the economic picture. But
surprisingly, yet nevertheless true, modern secular states
are still under the spell of the religious picture. Thus, for example, the French constitution (1958) declares France to be
secular, but not before it declares France to be "indivisible."[5]
The same goes for the expression "indivisible nation" in the
American Pledge of Allegiance. In both cases the choice of
the expression "indivisible" is no accident. It has strong religious underpinnings—it is one of God's attributes that informs the picture of an indivisible France and an indivisible
United States as absolute entities without legitimate fractions. Thus no claim of secession is acceptable as legitimate
because these two entities have no legitimate fractions. To
compromise over the Union is to betray the Union in the
same way that the idolater betrays the oneness of God.

The religious picture fills politics with the idea that politics is a domain of human activity meant to protect a way
of life and give meaning to human life. It is the antithesis of
the economic picture, concerned with satisfying desires and
interests, not with meanings.

The two pictures—the religious and the economic—evince
two different sets of motivations to explain political life. The
economic picture, even if not strictly hedonic, still explains

human behavior in terms of satisfying preferences, whereas the religious picture brings the willingness for self-sacrifice into the picture. A key mistake in political thought lies in disregarding the workings of either of the two pictures, in the belief that only one of the pictures sustains politics.

Not just politics is in the grip of the two pictures, the religious and the economic; this also holds true for morality itself. Utilitarian morality is clearly subject to the economic picture. The competing Kantian morality that promotes absolute moral imperatives irrespective of their consequences is molded on the picture of absolute religious commandments. We are ambivalent in evaluating compromise precisely because we are in the grip of two imprecise, powerful, and irreconcilable pictures of both politics and morality.

Forbidden Trade-off between Scarcity and Sacredness

Economics deals predominantly with the allocation of scarce resources. I use "predominantly" advisedly, since economics should also deal with unemployment, a case where labor is not scarce (this in a way is Keynes's amendment to the view that economics is the science of scarce resources, and only scarce resources). There are two stages in the allocation of scarce resources: production and exchange. Production transforms the commodity, whereas exchange transfers the control over it. The point of an exchange is that different agents value different things, in terms of other things, differently: for me, one avocado is worth two apples, whereas for you it is worth four apples. So we can both be better off by exchanging things I value less for things you value more. If I give you my avocado for three apples, I am better off by one apple and you are better off by one apple. That is all too banal to be worth

26

spelling out. Not banal at all, of course, are the ways in which things would be allocated such that no one would be able to improve one's lot by further exchange. Getting to an optimal allocation is the concern of the economist.

However, a whole chain of thoughts and attitudes that I link to the religious picture of politics forbids various kinds of economic exchanges. I am concerned with cases in which the very exchange is taboo because there is something degrading, if not sacrilegious, in the implicit comparison of the things that stand for exchange. To exchange what is sacred for money is, in the religious picture, the most debasing of exchanges.

Money, being a universal medium of exchange, is the "lowest" common denominator of all things, so selling the sacred for money is debasing the sacred more than any other exchange. The point is that in every exchange there is an explicit comparison between the items being exchanged—what one thing is worth in terms of another. Money as a universal medium of exchange claims that anything can be compared to anything.

A distinction should be drawn between *incomparable* and *incommensurable*.[6] Two things are incommensurable if they cannot be compared in quantitative terms (as we compare heights, for example); two things are incomparable if there are no qualitative terms to compare them. Incomparable is an expression of high praise. The God of the monotheistic religions claims this status of being absolutely incomparable. Things devoted to the deity (i.e., sacred things) claim by implication a similar status of incomparability.

Extending the market model to all spheres of life makes everything comparable to everything else and thus potentially leads to insulting comparisons. Those who adhere to the economic picture might say that indeed it is this feature of money—the great equalizer in the marketplace—that those who criticize the market economy for creating inequality miss so terribly.

The celebrated fictional exchange—

> *Scott Fitzgerald.* The rich are different from you and me.
> *Ernest Hemingway.* Yes, they have more money[7]—

is, nevertheless, a telling anecdote.

Money is a great equalizer because it reduces many differences and distinctions to one commensurate dimension. It enables fewer privileges based on qualitative differences that are not for sale. Aristocracy in its heyday was such a society, until titles of nobility became available for sale to the aspiring rich. It is mainly the snob, argues the marketer, who promotes the view that money, as the great equalizer, breeds vulgarity and loss of sense of value by comparing the incomparable.

Oscar Wilde's hilarious exchange in *Lady Windermere's Fan* captures in a cartoonist's exaggerated way the main divide between the two pictures: the economic and the religious, or, in Wilde's language, between the cynics and the sentimentalist.

> *Lord Darlington.* What cynics you fellows are!
> *Cecil Graham.* What is a cynic?
> *Lord Darlington.* A man who knows the price of everything and the value of nothing.
> *Cecil Graham.* And a sentimentalist, my dear Darlington, is a man who sees an absurd value in everything, and doesn't know the market price of any single thing.[8]

The point of the whole discussion about forbidden tradeoffs is that sorting out the difference between compromises and rotten compromises is part of a larger scheme of rendering certain trade-offs as taboo. The psychology of taboo trade-off is addressed expertly by Alan Fiske and Philip Tetlock.[9] They try to identify the conditions under which we are likely to treat trade-offs as taboo.

In my view, the religious picture in general, and the religious picture of politics in particular, is the source of our sense of forbidden trade-offs. The economic picture, on the other hand, loosens the hold of the religious picture that renders trade-offs taboo. The claim that there is a taboo on trading what one holds sacred is riddled with ambiguity: the thing that is tabooed does not have to be the thing that is sacred; it might even be anathema. When Jews and Muslims taboo pork, they do not hold swine as sacred; what they hold sacred is the will of God as expressed in the prohibition against eating pork. Turning the swine into a taboo means that not eating pork trumps everything else. The observant is not allowed to eat a tiny piece of pork for the largest amount of anything else. It is no good telling the observant that if you eat a tiny bit of pork, you will receive all the chocolate you want. He should refuse the offer. Indeed he should refuse to eat the tiny bit of pork for all the treasures of the world.

Not eating pork is nonnegotiable or almost so. (In Judaism one is allowed to eat pork to save one's life. Refraining from eating pork in Judaism does not trump saving one's life.) My point, however, is that taboo has the logic of a trumping relation. Even the tiniest piece of A should not be exchanged for the biggest amount of B.[10] We may distinguish between relative and absolute taboos. A is a relative taboo with regard to a particular kind of B if A trumps B (no tiny bit of A is allowed to be traded off for a huge chunk of B.) An absolute taboo is a taboo that stands in this relation to everything else.

Now that the framing of the issue of taboo trade-off is within view, I shall contrast the attitude of the two pictures in greater detail with an eye to their historical changes.

CHAPTER 1

What Should Money Not Buy?

Here is a celebrated example from *The Merchant of Venice*: Antonio receives a loan from Shylock, three thousand ducats for three months; should he fail to repay, Shylock is entitled to cut a pound of his flesh, in what part of the body he chooses. Flesh for money is taboo. In Shakespeare's play, however, quite surprisingly, Antonio, who has in the past humiliated Shylock (spat in public upon his "Jewish gabardine"), finds Shylock's offer generous, since Shylock does not charge him interest on the loan. ("I'll seal to such bond, And say there is much kindness in the Jew.")[11] For Antonio, usury, paying money on money, is abhorrent, but apparently not the mortgaging of flesh for money. We, however, are quite horrified by the deal. One can exchange meat for money but not one's flesh. Flesh, like other organs, can be donated for a good cause but not sold. I hasten to say that not all of us feel that way: libertarians think that there is nothing wrong in selling human organs. We are the owners of our bodies, and it is up to us to decide what to do with its parts.

The libertarian is not a cynic but is influenced by the economic picture to the extent that any transaction between consenting adults is allowed. We shall shortly meet the libertarian again.

For the Catholic Antonio, usury is an economic taboo; charging interest on loans is regarded nowadays as the core transaction of a market economy. So what is taboo in economic exchanges is subject to historical changes. Let me venture to explain the taboo on usury. I am not vouching for the validity of my explanation but only allude to the kind of explanation needed.

In a market economy, not being able to repay a loan might legally, in the worst case, result in bankruptcy. By contrast, in the Bible or Quran economy, being unable to repay a loan might have meant slavery. Already, merely asking for a loan meant not being able to be helped by one's family, and it was a sign of the plight of being poor and surrounded by impoverished kith and kin. Aggravating the situation of the debtor by demanding interest was perceived as pushing the debtor toward slavery. If this is the right way to explain the source of the taboo on charging a fee on the use of money, we can see why the Quran considered usury as a pact with the devil: "Those who charge usury are in the same position as those controlled by the devil's influence" (Al-Baqarah 2:275). A loan should be a charitable act, a gift, not an economic exchange. A charitable gift should have only intrinsic value and should not be bought for money, since money is the embodiment of that which has only exchange value.

Religious blessing is a paradigmatic case of a charitable gift, and a charitable gift is not for sale. Note the following exchange taken from Acts 8:

> 8:18. And when Simon saw that, by the imposition of the hands of the apostles, the Holy Ghost was given, he offered them money,
>
> 8:19. Saying: Give me also this power, that on whomsoever I shall lay my hands, he may receive the Holy Ghost. But Peter said to him:
>
> 8:20. Keep thy money to thyself, to perish with thee: because thou hast thought that the gift of God may be purchased with money.

Indeed, simony, the crime of buying office in the church, is named after Simon Magus, who offered money in exchange for the power to bestow blessings. Simony and the abuse of indulgence (remission of temporal punishment for money) became the symbols of religious corruption: sale of salvation for money. ("As soon as the coin in the coffer rings, a soul from purgatory springs.") Luther made a major grievance of the abuse of this kind of worldly transaction, debasing what has intrinsic value by turning it into exchange value.

All this is pure religion, but here is a dramatic political example of a heated public debate centered on the issue of taboo trade-off shaped by the religious view of politics. The transaction was memory of blood for money. On September 10, 1952, Israel and West Germany signed an accord, the Reparations Agreement, according to which Germany had to pay Israel for their persecution of the Jews during the Holocaust.

Before and after the signature of the agreement, nothing divided the Jews in Israel more than the Reparations Agreement. It was only seven years after the destruction of European Jewry, and the nightmarish memory of the war was still as haunting as ever. The great advocate of the agreement was David Ben-Gurion; his opposition came from both the Left and the Right. One of the arguments in favor of the agreement was couched in the biblical saying "Have you murdered and also taken possession?" The source of this saying is the story of Naboth the Jezreelite (1 Kings 21), who refused to sell his vineyard to Ahab and was killed by a plot hatched by Jezebel, Ahab's wicked wife, which resulted in her husband's taking possession of the vineyard. The prophet Elijah then admonished Ahab with God's words "Have you murdered and also taken possession?" The analogy meant not only that Nazi Germany had killed the Jews, but also that they should not be allowed to enjoy the stolen Jewish property without providing compensation. On this account, the trade-off is compensation for possession and for the harm done to the enslaved Jewish laborers in the Nazi machine, and not forgiveness for the murder of six million Jews. The point was that no trade-off taboo was violated. The opposition from the Right, led by Menachem Begin, proclaimed the slogan "Our honor shall not be sold for money. Our blood shall not be atoned for goods. We shall erase the shame."[12] Selling the memory of the murdered for money: that's how the opposition depicted the Reparations Agreement.

The Libertarian and the Cynic View of What Is Rotten

In the libertarian view, any agreement and any transaction among consenting adults that does not vitiate the rights of third parties is never morally rotten. Compromise as a clear case of agreement between consenting adults is never rotten, if it leaves the rights of third parties intact. Consenting adults may agree on incestuous relations, on selling and buying human organs, on polygamy and bondage sex, on selling and buying sex, drugs, and what not—none of those is in and of itself morally objectionable, so long as the rights of third parties are not infringed. The libertarian admits that some people, perhaps most people, may find some or most of the above repulsive, but one should not confuse aesthetic revulsion with moral scruple. The libertarian, advocating rugged individualism, is interested chiefly in individual transactions rather than in collective agreements. But I guess that the same idea holds collectively for them, and agreement and any compromise among consenting collectives are acceptable as long as they are not at the expense of third parties—whether individuals or a collective. The libertarian does not push the economic picture to its limit; he disapproves of agreements that trample the rights of third parties against their will. A rotten compromise, in the libertarian view, can occur only in an agreement carried out at the expense of the rights of third parties. And just as between consenting adults, anything goes between willing collectives, and there are no taboos on trade-off.

To a willing person no injury is done, says the Latin maxim (*Volenti non fit injuria*), consenting bystanders included. This holds true for a boxer badly injured in a fight, who had expressly agreed to inflict and suffer pain; it is also true for a spectator at a baseball game who cannot complain if a ball hits him while he sits in the bleachers: the spectator is, within reason, a consenting spectator.

For the cynic who fits Wilde's definition there are no rotten compromises, only good and bad deals; the language of rights prominent in the arsenal of the libertarian does not belong in the vocabulary of the cynic. There are many cynics in practice but only few, if any at all, in ideology. There are few libertarians in ideology, and even fewer in practice.

For our topic, the libertarian should address two questions: Would he accept a pact of consenting adults that establishes master-slave relations between them? Would the libertarian accept a pact between a consenting Marquis de Sade and a Leopold von Sacher-Masoch, to establish a regime of systematic humiliation and cruelty between them? In short, are slavery and a sadomasochistic free pact morally acceptable to the libertarian?

The libertarian may, whimsically yet tellingly, say that he accepts a slavery pact even though he regards it as utterly perverse, given that the highest value in human life should be freedom. But the libertarian may add that even a nonlibertarian text, the Hebrew Bible, allows consenting slavery on the part of someone who declares, "I love my master."

The case of a permanent voluntary slavery pact is in our world rather fanciful. However, radical feminists may describe women staying in oppressive marriages as not unlike the biblical Hebrew slave who declares, "I love my master," not out of love to the master himself, but out of love for his own wife and children.[13]

They may shy away from faulting the women in such cases, yet they view a semivoluntary marriage pact as rotten. They would argue that woman's oppression in marriage is the primordial form of oppression, and the base for all other forms of oppression; slavery is only one historical form of such oppression; the oppression of the slave woman in the biblical example says it all. In such radical feminist views, the family is a political entity that makes the marriage agreement rotten, not only a personally rotten pact, but also a politically rotten pact. I don't know whether any radical feminist has used this rather far-fetched analogy, but I can see that a radical feminist would not find it so far-fetched.

A libertarian, who speaks in the name of freedom as the ultimate value in human life, is to my mind in a double bind. He may bite the bullet and say that if someone freely gives his consent to a pact of slavery, one has to accept it, even if slavery is the denial of the ultimate value. Or he may say that since his moral system is predicated on adult free consent, slavery that renounces free consent thus renounces the basis on which the libertarian system is erected. So for the sake of retaining a system based on adult consent, no adult consent can be given to giving up adult consent, which is what slavery is.

The psychology of sadomasochistic practices is hard to understand, and its phenomenology not easily accounted for. In my opinion, the question whether to label a voluntary sadomasochistic pact a rotten compromise depends not on whether it is voluntary, but on whether it establishes a systematic practice of cruelty and humiliation between the parties to the pact. The overt features of the practice seem that way— systematic infliction of serious pain accompanied by overt gestures of humiliation. Yet there is a distinct feeling that an S&M pact, a pact limited in time, is actually a charade. Indeed, the element of charade is what turns the sadomasochistic deal into a compromise.

The inflicted pain is real enough; it is not, however, an expression of cruelty but rather an intense, if perverse, erotic arousal. The gestures of humiliation, in turn, are more a parody than an expression of cruelty. The relations of domination and submission expressed in such meetings are in the final analysis controlled by the submissive and the humiliated ones. They can stop it whenever they wish. And this is the compromise.

In short, revolting as these practices appear to most of us, they do not amount to a regime of cruelty and humiliation, and their meaning (if this is the word) is misconstrued if they are taken as such. So the question is: how serious is the practice of S&M? Seriousness, here, is not measured by pain. What makes it serious is the meaning of the pain. The question then is this: is the S&M practice an expression of cruel humiliation, or is it a mock expression of cruel humiliation, for erotic satisfaction?

The libertarian is indifferent to my question. He makes up his mind and decides that if the practice is between consenting adults, it is not rotten. For me, if the practice is indeed a manifestation of cruelty and humiliation, it is rotten even if agreed upon by consenting adults, whether in personal relations, or in collective relations.

Two Observations

The economic picture of politics is framed by two very broad observations: one by Hume and the other by Adam Smith.

Hume's observation starts with a reminder. Look at nature and see how lions fare in comparison to human beings. Lions have bodies impressively adapted to their life—they are majestically strong and remarkably agile—whereas we naked apes called humans look quite pathetic. Yet in the animal kingdom humans and not lions are kings.[14]

What accounts for this brilliant human success? Hume's answer is that humans, unlike lions, are wonderfully capable of cooperating in many varied and flexible ways: leonine cooperation, unlike human cooperation, is rigidly confined to a few tasks. In the language of Hume, human cooperation is artificial, based on dispositions sensitive to social conventions, and not on fixed innate dispositions that Hume calls natural. The artificial disposition to cooperate, which may vary from society to society, requires trust. Trust is enshrined in the institution of promise, which in turn is the cement of social life. Compromise, which etymologically derives from co-promises or mutual promises, is cooperation based on mutual promises.

Smith's observation is as follows: human beings compete over goods produced out of scarce resources. Competition means that agents who strive to gain scarce goods cannot all have them to their full satisfaction. Scarcity is a necessary condition for competition. Scarce but undesirable objects are not subject to competition. We desire diamonds, or at least some of us do. We do not desire ashes. In the absence of any desire for ashes, even in a world that holds small amounts of them, ashes go to ashes—they are not subject to competition as diamonds are. Ashes may be rare without being scarce. Rarity is a fact of nature; scarcity is a social fact. Scarcity is what turns something into an economic or a political good—a good subject of competition. Competition is built into the very idea of economic and political goods.

Hume's and Smith's observations are far-reaching and vague. They were not the first to make these observations, but perhaps the first to understand their full implication: namely, that the fundamental problem of human political life is how to address the tension between cooperation and competition: compromise is an essential element in relieving this tension.

A Very Short Summary

A helpful map not only gives you the layout of the land but tells you with a conspicuous sign, "You are here." So where are we? We are grappling with two pictures of politics: the religious picture and the economic picture. From the religious picture we get a strong sense that some things are not exchangeable. There is an absolute taboo on some transactions. I gave various examples of such taboo trade-offs, mostly dealing with money as a debasing medium of exchange. Some are directly related to religious practices, and others are inspired by religious practices.

The idea of rotten compromises as compromises that should be subjected to absolute taboos ties in with this picture. The economic picture sanctions no exchanges in absolute terms. In this view, there exist irrational exchanges, but when performed voluntarily by responsible adults, all such exchanges are allowed; none are absolutely taboo.

So where are we on this map? When the map is politics, we are left with one absolute taboo on exchanges. Its contours will be drawn in the next chapter.

-2-

Varieties of Compromise

A CURIOUS PUZZLE arises here. The notion of compromise hardly ever appears in the most elaborate conceptual account of the relation between competition and cooperation, namely, game theory.[1] Compromise has two meanings: anemic and sanguine. The anemic sense is covered by game theory, though not under the name "compromise"; the sanguine one is not. In the anemic sense of compromise, any agreement within a bargaining range is a compromise.

Abraham wants to buy a burial place from Ephron (Genesis 23:7–9). Let us assume that the worth of the burial site is 450 silver shekels for Abraham and 200 silver shekels for Ephron. Any agreement between 200 and 450 shekels is beneficial to both (cooperation). But different possible agreements in this range benefit each differently (competition). The range between 200 and 450 is the bargaining range and consists of a set of *feasible agreements*. Abraham the buyer wants to keep the price close to 200, whereas Ephron the seller wants to keep it as close to 450 as possible. Abraham is hard-pressed: he must bury his beloved wife Sarah quickly. Ephron can afford to be patient, but he is afraid that if he insists too long, someone else may offer Abraham a better deal. The Bible tells us that the deal was struck at 400 silver shekels. The bargaining between Ephron and Abraham requires two comparisons from the two players. One compares feasible agreements among themselves, and one compares what would happen if they do not reach an agreement, to *the point of conflict.*[2] There is another implicit comparison to possible outside deals: what could Ephron get for his plot from other buyers, and what would Abraham have to pay for a plot from other sellers?

We may call any agreement within the bargaining range (200–450) a compromise: in this reading of compromise, the anemic reading, the bargaining theory as a branch of game theory covers this sense of compromise. I am interested in a more sanguine sense of compromise. Our daily nonsystematic use of the term "compromise" fits the sanguine sense better than the anemic sense. However, some ordinary uses of the term do fit the anemic sense.

I refer to the phenomenology of sanguine compromise and wonder whether game theory can accommodate it as part of the logic of bargaining. Something similar happened to the familiar phenomenology of competition in neoclassical economic theory: perfect competition was rendered so perfect that all the features associated with competition—reducing prices, saving costs, making your product distinctive, hiring and firing—faded away.

There is too much sanguine compromise in our life—even with the perception that there is not enough of it—to leave it unaccounted for. But more to the point: it is the sanguine sense of compromise that is pertinent to morality. So I repeat: an anemic compromise between you and me over X is any agreement between us within the range of what X is worth to you and what X is worth to me. A sanguine compromise over X is an anemic compromise with additional features, the most important being recognition.

Sanguine Compromise: Recognition

A clear case of sanguine compromise strongly suggests (rather than implies) recognizing the point of view of the other. Compromise may be an expression of such recognition. It confers legitimacy on the point of view of the other side. Sanguine compromise may even involve a measure of sacrifice from the strong side, not driving as hard a bargain as it could to get what it desires. The point of such sacrifice is indeed to confer recognition on one's rival and to dispel an image of domination. By meeting the other party halfway, one may suggest a semblance of equality between nonequals. Acting in such a spirit of compromise is what the Talmud calls acting for the sake of peace.

The Talmud distinguishes three types of reasons under the heading of acting "for the sake of peace," as distinct from acting "for the sake of justice (*din*)":

- Compromise to neutralize hostility
- Compromise to enhance harmony by reducing friction
- Compromise to indicate to your rival that you recognize the force and the legitimacy of his claim, even if you could win in a trial

It is that third category of acting for the sake of peace that is linked to the idea of recognition as a salient element of sanguine compromise.

In a stylized type of bargaining, the one following the idea of anemic compromise, the actors ("players") are clear. Also usually clear are the various feasible agreements that they can achieve. However, the phenomenology of political bargaining suggests that a great deal of compromise is needed to influence the parties (the actors, the players) as well as to determine the feasible agreements.

41

By the pompous term "phenomenology" I mean no more than a description of the central features of compromises, implicit in our practices, even before we are aware of any theory about it.

The phenomenology of political compromise suggests that one key form of compromise takes place when one recognizes the other side as a legitimate partner for negotiation. Sometimes, recognizing the other as a legitimate side for bargaining is harder than reaching an actual agreement. Recognition of the armed Basque separatists (ETA) by Spain, or the Shining Path by the government of Peru, or the Kurdistan Workers Party by Turkey, as partners for negotiations, is as difficult for Spain, Peru, and Turkey, respectively, as any concession they may be required to make in order to reach an agreement.

Dubbing the other party "a terrorist organization" is tantamount to regarding them as illegitimate partners—as extortionists who should be resisted. Removing an organization from a "terrorist list" and making it one side of a negotiation is usually a major concession from the party that confers legitimacy. The legitimizing side in return expects a major concession from the "former terrorist organization."

Thus compromise may take place *on the way to* the negotiation rather than *in* the negotiation. It takes place when the two sides recognize each other. Recognizing a mortal enemy, hitherto unrecognized, as a legitimate party of negotiation may play a transformative role in humanizing the enemy, and in acknowledging the enemy as holding legitimate concerns. It calls for empathy—an attentive effort to understand the enemy's concerns from the enemy's point of view. It calls for empathy and not for sympathy (identification with the enemy concerns).

The point here is deep: negotiation is meant to bring about cooperation, so recognizing the other as a party for negotiation acknowledges that the other party is worthy of coopera-tion. By cooperating with you, I am committed to increase both our shares, not just my own share. I am, of course, inter-ested in my share, but cooperation means the recognition that I cannot increase my share without increasing yours.[3] If I de-cide to cooperate after a bitter conflict, it means that I give up on belligerence: I give up on my effort to decrease your share. Yet it does not necessarily mean that I give up competing with you: trying to increase the difference between my share and yours. The spirit of sanguine compromise, unlike the simply anemic one, is more than striving to cooperate. It is a con-certed effort by both of us to reduce competition, that is, the difference between us. My pursuing a sanguine compromise with you does not in any way mean that I am swept by a spirit of altruism, whereby all I care about is how to increase your share for your sake. This may happen when I negotiate with my children, not with you. But there may be an element of sacrifice in sanguine compromise, deliberately decreasing my share compared to possible agreements that I might have ex-tracted, had I insisted. I want only to express my goodwill and commitment to cooperation rather than competition, in the hope that my sacrifice will be appreciated and reciprocated in the long run, thereby holding the agreement stable.

We should distinguish between two aspects of bargaining. One is a compromise *on the frame* of the negotiation. The other is the compromise *in the* negotiation, once the setup for the negotiations is agreed upon. A sanguine compromise *on the frame* of the negotiation that involves recognizing the other as a legitimate partner for negotiation means treating the other less as an enemy and more as a rival. The meaning of sanguine compromise *in the* negotiation is narrowing down the rivalry. With a rival, the stress is on competing for the same object; with an enemy, the stress is on the desire to harm the enemy.

Bargaining concentrates on the bone of contention, whereas a conflict of violent hostility concentrates on breaking the backbone of the enemy. The issue in bargaining is not how to turn *enemy* into *friend* but how to turn *enemy* into *rival*.

In any case, being deemed worthy of cooperation is a major political recognition. A move from nonrecognition to recognition can constitute a major concession: if properly reciprocated, it constitutes a sanguine compromise. The hope is that all this talk about the role of recognition in negotiation remains true as long as the negotiation is not conducted under duress. Negotiating with hijackers, kidnappers, and extortionists does not amount to recognizing the others as legitimate partners for cooperation, but only yielding to the coercive threat as the lesser evil. But the strong suggestion that negotiation is a form of recognition deters legitimate regimes from negotiating even under duress with blackmailers.[4]

At the core of serious sanguine political compromise is a dispute that involves more than interests, narrowly conceived. Beside interests, it involves principles and ideals (moral, political, aesthetic, religious). What is negotiated in serious disputes is sometimes the self-identity of the sides to the dispute. By "identity" I mean not reputation in the eyes of others but self-identification. A serious sanguine compromise involves not just recognition of the other but also self-recognition. This is the sense in which Marshal Pétain was accused in his trial, that by concluding an armistice agreement with the Nazis, he compromised the historical identity of France.

Sanguine Compromise: Giving Up on a Dream

In shaping the bargaining scene, determining the parties for negotiation and determining the set of feasible agreements may involve a major compromise, a sanguine one. I have so far mentioned the compromise that involves recognizing the parties to negotiation. But determining the feasible agreement on the basis of which a solution could be found may call for important compromises from the negotiating parties, especially in the case of historically loaded political disputes.

Classical stylized bargaining is based on comparison between a feasible agreement and a point of conflict (nonagreement). The point of nonagreement usually means reverting to the status quo, perhaps with the addition of the bad blood of failed negotiation, and not reaching an agreement. However, in collective conflicts, especially conflicts with ideological overtones and emotional undertones, we find an explicit or implicit comparison to another point of reference external to the feasible set of agreements—not a meeting point but a *dream point*.[5]

Let me use as an example a conflict close to my heart and constantly on my mind: Israel and the Palestinians. It cries out to the two elements of sanguine compromise *on the frame* of the negotiation before even talking of compromise in the negotiation itself. First, there was the issue of recognition, which for a while seemed to be resolved, but which reverted to the status quo.

For the Palestinians, the issue was to recognize what they consider an illegitimate "Zionist entity" as the legitimate State of Israel. For Israel, the issue was to recognize the illegitimate "terrorist organization," the PLO and its leader Yasser Arafat, as the legitimate representatives of the Palestinian people, which could negotiate their legitimate interests.[6]

This deals with the compromise regarding the parties to the bargaining. But the two sides still disagree about what should be included in the set of feasible agreements. The external comparison that the two sides engage in is not to a point of conflict—the lack of agreement. The external comparison that the two sides are engaged in concerns their respective dream points: these points are nonstarters for negotiation, even as an extreme opening position. Each side measures the concession required not in relation to the conflict point, but rather in relation to its dream. Indeed, a politically important form of sanguine compromise is for both sides to give up on their "dreams" so that what remains to negotiate is a range of possible agreements.

On the face of it, compromising a dream is not real compromise, since no tangible concessions are involved, only a fantasy. Usually the two sides in a dispute treat each other's dream very differently. Your dream is just a dream with no prospect of coming true, so you sacrifice nothing in giving that dream up; you only free yourself from an illusion to better cope with reality. I do not consider your giving up on your dream as a serious concession, whereas giving up on my dream is sacrificing something that admittedly may not be implemented now, but which, with stamina and determination, may be achievable in the long run. If, however, I do give up on the dream for the sake of alleviating the suffering of my generation, it should be counted as a major concession.

This familiar double standard of literally treating the other's dream as a mere illusion, and one's own dream as a possible aspiration point, renders sanguine concessions on the range of feasible agreements very difficult.

The dream point plays another important role in bargaining, because that dream serves to shape the identity of the community when it focuses on its implementation. The dream is a constitutive element in the identity of a historical community.

To compromise on a dream is interpreted by the hardliners in the community as giving up the identity of the group, and thus as an act of betrayal. The hard-liners try to confer on the dream the status of the sacred. On occasion, the hard-liners prevail and the dream is perceived by the community as a whole as sacred, and as nonnegotiable. Dreams may be considered merely as tribal tom-tom drums, which appeal to the tribe and to no one else. But each tribe translates its dreams into entitlements. In territorial disputes, the entitlement claim may be couched in terms of historical rights to the place—we were there first, or the place is essential to our self-understanding as a community because of the historical events that happened here. The force of the historical rights claim, even if it carries weight only for the claimants, does not make giving it up easy. One side's giving up on it, even partially, for the sake of peace should not be ignored by the other side. It should be regarded as a major sanguine compromise, to be reciprocated by the other side's giving up on its own dream. This holds if the claims of entitlements are credible and not mere sham commitments later to be dropped, so as to increase one's share. But how can one tell the difference between sham commitment and real commitment? One indication of the seriousness of the dream is whether enough believe that their side can go all out and get the whole hog for themselves. Trying to get it all may be a mad and dangerous gamble, yet if enough people believe that with stamina, sacrifice, and true grit they can have it all, with no need to share, then giving up on a dream is all the more serious; the dream verges on being an aspiration point—an expected payoff.

It is precisely the belief that one can have it all for oneself which encourages the view that compromise is surrender. If, for instance, one can have the greater Israel, or the greater Palestine, by blood and fire, then any compromise based on partition of land will bring the accusation of surrender and betrayal.

More Features of Sanguine Compromise

Mutual Concessions

Every sanguine compromise must be based on mutual concessions: on splitting the difference. This is not true for all anemic compromises. If Abraham and Ephron end up with Abraham paying the full price for the burial site—450 silver shekels—we would view it as an agreement, and by definition as an anemic compromise. Yet the deal between them is not a sanguine compromise. Anyone confronted with a fixed price on a product in a store, "take it or leave it," may take it, but we hardly call that a compromise, meaning that it is not a sanguine compromise.

The proverbial case of sanguine compromise is meeting *halfway*: in our case, dividing by two the difference (250) between what the site is worth to Abraham (450) and what it is worth to Ephron (200); in the proverbial sanguine compromise, Abraham would have paid Ephron 325 silver shekels. On a proverbial compromise, the relative strength of the two sides in bargaining is ignored. Meeting halfway may, of course, be the result of an anemic compromise, but only if the two sides are comparable in their bargaining strength. However, a proverbial compromise of meeting halfway does not assume that the two are symmetrical. A sanguine compromise is not necessarily the proverbial compromise of meeting halfway, yet it does mean splitting the difference not too far from some central value.

Thomas Schelling writes: "'Bargaining power', 'bargaining strength', 'bargaining skill' suggests that the advantage goes to the powerful, the strong, or the skillful. It does, of course, if those qualities are defined to mean only that negotiations are won by those who win. But if the terms imply that it is an advantage to be more intelligent or more skilled in debate, or to have more financial resources, more physical strength, more military potency, or more ability to withstand losses, then the term does a disservice. These qualities are by no means universal advantages in the bargaining situation; they often have a contrary value."[7]

Schelling is right to say that conventional qualities like financial resources, military potency, and intelligence do not always provide an advantage during bargaining. He is wrong to suggest that, therefore, bargaining power is an empty concept backed merely by a tautology: the stronger party in the negotiation is the one that wins the negotiation.

I am willing to bet that in most negotiations, the side with the conventional qualities of strength gets a larger share than the side that lacks them. Not always, true, but far more often than not. Would Schelling deny that? A conventionally strong side in negotiation may recognize cases in which it has to make concessions to the weak just because it is weak. For example, it may be in its best interest to make the weak side relatively strong by means of the negotiation, to avoid facing an unyielding side. This is familiar, but familiar does not mean that it is the most common occurrence.

The case we were interested in is that in which the conventionally strong side makes concessions to the conventionally weak side so as to give the negotiation a semblance of dealing with equals—namely, as a token of recognition. If this happens, then I would regard it as a case of sanguine compromise, even if the weak side cannot reciprocate in kind, but recognizes the meaning of the gesture, and makes other kinds of concessions, the concessions of the weak.

The concept of mutual concessions is quite straightforward; the psychology involved is complicated. We tend to regard our own concessions as real sacrifices and minimize the concessions of the other side. It is what behavioral economists dub the "endowment effect": the effect of enhancing the value of our endowment relative to what it is when in the hands of others.[8] This is partly why doves find it difficult to sell a compromise, being exposed—as they always are—to a charge by the hawks, "You are not engaged in a compromise but in capitulation; the other side is not making significant concessions."

Does compromise always require something like splitting the difference? Not quite. There is a notion that views the essence of compromise not so much in splitting the difference as in the willingness to accept a redescription of what is in dispute. For example, if Jews and Muslims would agree to redescribe their dispute about sovereignty over the Temple Mount in Jerusalem in terms of a dispute about the *use* of the place, then the main compromise step is already taken; splitting the *use* is trivial, whereas splitting sovereignty is extremely hard.

Deadlock

In ordinary usage, we hardly use the word "compromise" to cover all transactions. It would be odd to describe buying a bottle of milk at a fixed price in a supermarket as a compromise. Compromise, in general, is perceived as a response to a fairly serious matter. A paradigmatic case of compromise is a response to a deadlock in negotiation. Breaking a genuine deadlock would be rendered in the ordinary use of the term as a clear case of a compromise, especially if the two sides made discernible concessions to break the deadlock.

A clear case of a sanguine compromise is that of breaking a deadlock by mutual concessions, splitting the difference. Breaking a deadlock by having one side make all the concessions is hardly a sanguine compromise. A deadlock that can be broken by a compromise is one in which the agents at first genuinely do not know what they prefer: to insist on their aspiration point ("the dream"), to retreat to the conflict point and do nothing, or to carry on with the negotiation.

A deadlock, even one that leads to bloody conflict, is not necessarily an indication that no agreement point exists between the two rivals. The more costly the conflict, the greater is the chance that there exists an agreement better than the bloody conflict.[9] We may add that by this logic, if there is a more feasible and a better agreement than the conflict point, then there is more than one such point. So a deadlock may occur when there is more than one feasible agreement rather than none at all.

But how can two agents involved in a deadlock leading to a bloody conflict be considered rational? Given that not reaching an agreement is perilous and the conflict point is bloody, it must be the case that an agreement exists which is better than no agreement. So how can the two sides fail to reach an agreement and still be viewed as rational?

One trite yet true answer is that it can happen if the two are locked in a situation of inbuilt rational mistrust, say, of a prisoner's dilemma type, in which neither believes that the other will keep the agreement. Another possibility is to argue that it can happen if the two rivals face different agreements that favor the two parties in very unequal ways: each agent rationally prefers the agreement that works in its favor. In certain circumstances, it might perhaps be rational for each to try to fake strengths and hide vulnerabilities so as to push the other to accept their favorite agreement, even at the risk of war. This is not as simple as it sounds. Rational bargaining theory presents the set of all feasible agreements between two competing rivals as a convex set.[10] This means that any weighted average point between two possible agreement points is also an agreement open to the two. So how can rational agents fail to reach an intermediary compromise point rather than end in a bloody war? This is quite a puzzle to those who try to give a rational explanation of wars—at least of some wars.

My underlying concern is not with the rationality of wars but with their morality. It deals not with the question of how two rivals can end up in war and still be regarded as rational, but rather with Thomas Aquinas's question: is it always sinful to go to war? Given my concern, I would like to highlight two worries related to the possibility of a deadlock that will loom large in chapter 3: the politics of the holy and the fear of irredentism.

One tactical move in bargaining is painfully familiar: to make a commitment to a demand that leaves very little room for compromise, thus forcing the other side to accept your terms. Declaring your soil holy is one way of making a strong commitment in negotiation. "Our land does not yield itself to bargaining. It is not even open to argument. To us, the national soil is equal to the holy valley where God Almighty spoke to Moses." The speaker of these words was Anwar Sadat, the president of Egypt, in the Israeli parliament on November 20, 1977.[11]

The holy sometimes creeps into profane politics as a tactical commitment, but the language of the holy is not tactical; it has a life of its own. Its use makes it very hard to revoke one's commitments; the cost of revoking a commitment when the holy is invoked is so high that it may lead to deadlock and to war rather than to compromise. Thank God, if this is an apt expression, Sadat succeeded in his gamble. But playing with the language of the holy is literally playing with fire. That is one worry.

Another worry is the fear of future irredentism—making territorial claims in the future that undermine the agreement. The fear of irredentism, that your partner to the agreement won't keep his side of the bargain, may paralyze the two sides into a deadlock.

In any case, breaking a genuine deadlock through an effort from both sides is a sure sign that the compromise is sanguine.

Noncoercion

A clear case of a sanguine compromise is when concessions made for the sake of compromise are not extracted by coercion. The coercion I have in mind is the coercion of one side to the agreement by the other side. Coercion involves a credible threat. A threat amounts to coercion if *all* the options that the threatened party faces are noticeably worse than *all* the options it faced before the threat was made. There are endless epicycles in the literature on this crude condition of coercion, but crude as it is, it is good enough for our needs.[12]

There are four cases to distinguish:

- *One*, the two sides agree that they should compromise and make mutual concessions, but the split between them is coerced. Accepting arbitration can take this form, yet it does not vitiate the idea that arbitration can end in a compromise.
- *Two*, the two sides are coerced by a third party, or one side is coerced by the other side to compromise, but the mutual concessions required from each side are left open to negotiation.
- *Three*, the case when not only the requirement for mutual concessions is imposed, but also the extent of the concessions is imposed. If ex post the two parties willingly accept the imposition, I still regard it as a compromise; if they do not, then it is not a compromise.
- *Four*, a third party coerces only one side to the dispute (say, its client state) to reach a compromise. This does not

preclude the agreement reached between the two sides from being regarded as a compromise, even though the main reason for the coerced party to accept the compromise is the coercive threat by the third party.

The four cases of coercion that I just listed are cases where coercion and compromise may happen together. This should not undermine the claim that the central cases of compromise, what I call clear cases, are cases of agreements free from coercion. Coercion goes in degrees; the distance of a given agreement from central cases of compromise depends, among other things, on how free the agreement is.

So a clear case of a sanguine compromise is an agreement (co-promise) that involves painful recognition of the other side, the giving up of dreams, making mutual concessions that express recognition of the other's point of view, and that is not based on coercion of one side by the other. If this is a sanguine compromise, what, then, is a rotten compromise? Especially, when is compromise rotten because of its content and not because of the nature of the compromisers?

I shall address these two questions with a short elucidation and a long illustration.

Was the Great Compromise a Rotten Compromise?

A rotten compromise is a compromise. It is an agreement that establishes or maintains an inhuman political order based on systematic cruelty and humiliation as its permanent features; usually the party that suffers the cruelty and the humiliation is not a party to the agreement. By humiliation, I mean dehumanization—treating humans as nonhumans. By cruelty I mean a pattern of behavior that willfully causes pain and distress. A rotten compromise that establishes or maintains an inhuman regime of cruelty and humiliation is an assault on morality itself, and that is what makes it radically evil.

The institution of slavery is a clear case of humiliation and cruelty. Slavery based on racism is doubly at fault, for one is degraded as a human being, both on account of being a slave and on account of one's race. So let me deal with compromises involving slavery as a test case for my account of a rotten compromise as one that consists in establishing or condoning the infliction of cruelty and humiliation.

It looks ridiculously anachronistic to charge the Mesopotamian king Hammurabi with adopting slavery as a basic institution some four thousand years ago. But there is nothing anachronistic in holding Jefferson accountable for his acceptance of slavery: abolition was for him a live option. A live option is not necessarily the preferred option. It is an option that is on the horizon of its members, especially if a significant number of members of the society, or in their immediate vicinity, opt for it. There is no question that during the formation of the Union, abolitionism was a live option.

In my view, a historical society is morally accountable relative to its live options. This does not mean that the wrongness— say, of slavery—is relative; but only that moral accountability is. So asking whether the United States was founded on a rotten compromise in accepting slavery is not an anachronistic question. The issue here, unlike the issue in the case of the Munich agreement, is the content of the compromise rather than who signed it. As a matter of fact, the agreement was signed by exceptionally remarkable individuals.

What enabled the formation of the Union and the acceptance of the American Constitution by its framers was the Connecticut compromise, hailed as the Great Compromise.

The person chiefly responsible for devising the compromise was Roger Sherman, celebrated as the "great compromiser." The two thorny issues that the compromise was meant to settle were political representation and slavery. The sticky issue for us is the compromise on slavery; slavery was recognized (though Madison succeeded in keeping the word "slave" out of the wording of the Constitution). The Constitution did not ban slavery; moreover, it did not empower Congress to do so. The importation of slaves was authorized until 1808.

Article 4, section 2, of the U.S. Constitution is particularly hideous. It orders that slaves who succeeded in escaping to free states be returned to their owners.[13]

The extent of the recognition of slavery came to the fore in the Missouri Compromise of 1820. In 1787, Congress had passed a law that banned slavery north of the Ohio River. When Missouri was about to be admitted as a state, the issue of whether to admit it as a slave state or as a free state was hotly contested, since parts of Missouri are north of the Ohio River. The compromise: Missouri was allowed to enter as a slave state and Maine as a free state.

This was the situation faced by the fiery abolitionist William Lloyd Garrison. Here are some of his sayings:

- "The abolitionism which I advocate is as absolute as the laws of God, and as unyielding as his throne. It admits of no compromise."[14]
- "I will be harsh as truth, and as uncompromising as justice. On this subject . . . I will not retreat a single inch."[15]
- "The compact which exists between the North and the South is a covenant with death and an agreement with hell."[16]

And then he made the statement that "with the North, the preservation of the Union is placed above all other things—above honor, justice, freedom, integrity of soul."[17]

The Union is for Garrison "the latest and the most terrible form of idolatry"; by that, he presumably meant that the Union, which he regarded as at most something of instrumental political value, had been turned into something of ultimate value. The Union was perceived by its adherents not solely in instrumental terms but as a moral ideal of great moment—"a more perfect union," a political order that would be not just more efficient but morally better. Even as a schoolchild in faraway Jerusalem I understood, as we read Stephen Vincent Benét's classic "The Devil and Daniel Webster," that when Webster keeps asking from his grave, "Neighbor, how stands the Union?" he is echoing the belief that the Union is something much higher than a mere political arrangement: one can sell his soul to the devil for personal gain and still be defended by Webster, the greatest lawyer of his time, but no one can betray the Union and be defended.

Be that as it may, for Garrison the Constitution was a pact with the devil: a rotten compromise if ever there was one. Garrison had the sublimity of language, the fearless independence, and the spiritual nobility of a biblical prophet. But was he right? Was the Union based on a rotten compromise, one that enabled the Constitution to be accepted at the price of recognizing a political order that was systematically cruel and deeply humiliating to a distinct group of people?

The Constitution and the Union did not establish slavery. This in itself is a relevant fact, though not a decisive one, in the assessment of the agreement's rottenness. Establishing slavery is much worse. But the question we face is, did the agreement help maintain slavery? The historical verdict is, most likely not. It seems that in the final analysis the establishment of the Union did more to undermine slavery than to help maintain it.

This verdict is an empirical historical judgment, not a normative judgment.[18] However, what is morally relevant is this question: could one at the time the agreement was made predict in good faith that forming the Union was going to help the cause of abolishing slavery, rather than sustain the institution? The ultimate verdict on the compromise involved in forming the Union depends on such judgments. If the soundest judgment available to those who framed the "more perfect union" was that the Union was going to help maintain slavery rather than abolish it, then the compromise must be pronounced rotten. Indeed, there were better reasons for the framers of the American Constitution to believe that slavery was on its way out, and that the Union would hasten its ending, than it came to be reasonable to believe a few years later.

The framers might well have believed that slavery was on its way out because of Adam Smith's view that slavery was not just morally wrong but, in the long run, also economically inefficient: "It appears, accordingly, from the experience of all ages and nations, I believe, that the work done by free men comes cheaper in the end than the work performed by slaves. . . . Whatever work he does, beyond what is sufficient to purchase his own maintenance, can be squeezed out of him by violence only, and not by any interest of his own."[19] Moreover, there was good reason to believe that the slave states were more likely to recognize both the immorality of slavery and the economic case against the institution through interaction with the free states than through isolation.

The founding fathers could hardly know that a few years after the Constitution was forged, the cotton gin would be invented, speeding the separation of cotton from seedpod so as to turn cotton into an enormously profitable business. The production of cotton was massively increased, bringing a massive demand for slaves. However, once the cotton gin was in place, the force of the belief that slavery was on its way out had been weakened.

Be that as it may, the point is that in evaluating the compromise over slavery, as well as other compromises, we should pay attention only to the reasons believed ex ante (before the Constitution), rather than the reasons believed ex post (after the Constitution was agreed upon).

But what if in good faith and for good reasons they believed at the time that slavery was on its way out and that establishing the Union would help the cause of ending slavery more quickly? The answer should *not* automatically be "Well, this would absolve the compromise from being a rotten compromise." An added question should first be addressed: how long would it take for the compromise to produce the beneficial effect of ending slavery?

I suggest that the upper limit for the relevant time span should be a generation: the prospect of abolishing slavery within the frame of the Union should be within the horizon of a living generation. The reason is that one should morally reject the biblical notion of a "desert generation"—a generation whose life can be sacrificed for the sake of building a better future for the coming generations. (The "desert generation" gets its name from the generation that wandered with Moses in the desert only to die out before the next generation could enter the Promised Land.) Any revolutionary moral futurism that advocates sacrificing the revolutionary generation so as to enable future generations to enter a Promised Land should be discarded on the basis of my desert-generation test. In moral life the long run is the span of one's mature life.

My justification for the desert-generation test is fundamentally Kantian: we must not use humans merely as means to an end, even if the end can be morally praised, say, forming "the more perfect union" so as to emancipate slaves in the future. Members of a desert generation can give their consent and sacrifice themselves to create a better society in the future: to serve, as the slogan has it, as "oil in the wheel of a revolution." But no regime is entitled to impose such sacrifice on a generation without its consent.

In any case, no one asked, even implicitly, the black slaves whether they consented to the Constitution. Moreover, the interdiction on the importation of slaves after 1808 was not meant to free those already enslaved, and the Fugitive Slave Law helped strengthen owners' grip on the slaves of the desert generation.

The twenty-year span envisaged by the Constitution for a ban on the importation of slaves veered toward the limit of a generational span (given the life expectancy of slaves at the time). Madison was keenly aware of the span problem. "Twenty years will produce all the mischief that can be apprehended from the liberty to import slaves; so long a term will be more dishonorable to the National character than to say nothing about it in the Constitution."[20]

Yet he defended the compromise of the twenty-year clause by saying that in the old arrangement the importation of slaves was permitted forever. So in the end Madison did not accept the generation-span condition. He wanted us to compare the prospects of slaves to be freed under the Constitution to their prospects without the Constitution in order to assess whether the compromise was rotten "mischief." This violates my desert-generation criterion; a compromise should not be struck if it means accepting systematic cruelty and humiliation over the horizon of a generation. The 1808 clause pushed the desert-generation test to its limit.

Was the Constitution, then, an outcome of a rotten compromise?

Replying to this blunt question hinges on contested facts. I tried to supply, not a definite answer, but a way of thinking about the question.

However, I shall not duck the question. My tentative answer is that the Constitution was based on a rotten compromise. It was rotten not because it helped, in general, maintain an inhuman regime—it probably did not—but because it did help maintain an inhuman regime for a whole desert generation (indeed more than one). The restriction on importation of slaves after 1808 wouldn't, in any case, help the generation of those who were already slaves. My tentative tone of voice is due to the claim I have just made, namely, the facts of this dreary affair are still contested.

If the compromise that enabled the Constitution was rotten, what does it tell us about the Constitution as a whole?

Later in the book I make a distinction between two cases: a cockroach in the soup, and a fly in the ointment. A cockroach disqualifies the entire soup. A fly in the ointment disqualifies the ointment only partially. Given this distinction, the question is: was the Constitution a soup with a cockroach or an ointment with a fly? My short answer is that it was a soup, with slavery being a huge cockroach.

A rotten compromise over an item in an agreement infects an entire, otherwise agreeable agreement. More on this issue later.

Crimes against Humanity

When contemplating what renders compromises rotten, why single out cruelty and humiliation from among the many evils that popped out of Pandora's box? I single out the combination of humiliation and cruelty not only because we dread it most, which means not for reasons of welfare. My reason is constitutive: grave cruelty and humiliation undermine the notion of shared humanity.

Cruelty and humiliation go by degrees, as does the fusion of the two. The mild form of institutional humiliation makes for indecent society. But my sense of cruelty and humiliation is a much stronger notion than the mild notion of humiliation that serves to maintain an indecent society. The transition from mild forms of humiliation to a regime of cruelty and humiliation is meant to be a transition in kind, a transition from quantity to quality. In truth there is no such transition but only a continuum of cruelty and humiliation, which we somewhat artificially break. The idea is to create discontinuity by saying that at a certain point there is so much cruelty and humiliation that avoiding any further addition to it outranks any advantage one can get by accepting some alternative.

Had the expression "crimes against humanity" not been taken as a term of art, I would have used it as a better expression to convey my idea of a regime of systematic cruelty and humiliation. The claim then would have been expressed thus: a rotten compromise is a compromise that brings about or maintains crimes against humanity. Echoing article 6(c) of the charter that governed the Nuremberg trials, the International Criminal Court codified crimes against humanity: "'[C]rime against humanity' means any of the following acts when committed as part of a widespread or systematic attack directed against any civilian population, with knowledge of the attack: Murder; Extermination; Enslavement; Deportation or forcible transfer of population; Imprisonment or other severe deprivation of physical liberty . . . ; Torture;

Rape, sexual slavery, enforced prostitution . . . ; Enforced disappearance of persons; The crime of apartheid; other inhumane acts of a similar character intentionally causing great suffering, or serious injury to body or to mental or physical health."[21]

"Crime against humanity" is thus clearly a term of art. It is distinguished from war crimes and crimes of aggression, and applies equally in time of war and in time of peace. It does not distinguish among the humans against whom the crime is directed. It does not matter whether the victims belong to identified groups, as in the case of genocide. Crimes against humanity in the legal sense can be perpetrated only against civilian populations. I extend it to prisoners of war and to ex–prisoners of war, as my example of the forced repatriation of Soviet prisoners of war into Stalinist Russia at the end of the Second World War attests (chapter 4).

Crimes against humanity justify intervention on behalf of humanity against the perpetrators, even if that involves breaching the sovereignty of the state that commits the crime. My concern is different: it is not with active intervention but with passive abetting of such crimes through compromising deals.

Compromises should never be allowed in cases of crimes against humanity, except to save the lives of the people threatened by such regimes. I cannot overemphasize the reason why crimes against humanity are the ultimate taboo: they attack the very category on which morality is founded, that is, *shared humanity.*

I am making a distinction between *internal assault* and *external assault* on morality.

An analogy may clarify the distinction. Committing a flagrant foul—say, in basketball—is a bad thing to do. But bad as it is, the offender may be ejected from the game; it is still a violation within the game. By contrast, destroying the two baskets is destroying the game itself: it is not an illegitimate move in the game; it is a move against the very possibility of the game. The comparison between the two moves is not a comparison in degrees of nastiness; the difference is a difference in kind. Attacking the idea of shared humanity is like destroying the baskets. It is attacking a constitutive element of morality as the domain that should regulate all human relations. Excluding humans from the human race, thereby rendering them unfit for human relations, is an act of undermining morality. An intense form of racism is a paradigmatic case of an attack on the basic assumption of morality, which is shared humanity.

One reaction to the distinction between the internal and the external assault is this: ask the victims if they care a jot whether they are mistreated by a cruel regime that assaults morality as such, or by a regime that merely assaults them *within* morality. If the victims are indifferent to the distinction, the reaction goes on, then it is a distinction without merit.

This reaction is off the beam. The perspective of the victims, with regard to the distinction at hand, is the wrong perspective. Think of the distinction between murder and involuntary manslaughter, that is, between killing with malice aforethought and killing with no intent but out of recklessness. There is no doubt that this is a very important distinction morally and legally. But now ask the victims if they care one way or the other whether they are put to death by murder or by manslaughter. If you are troubled by the fact that in the case of murder or manslaughter there is no one to ask, then switch to those who survived death but remained paralyzed for life, and ask them if it matters to them which of the two kinds of action brought them the wretched affliction.

In a way, international law addresses our problem with rotten compromises: any agreement that encourages crimes against humanity is void under a peremptory norm (ius cogens) that absolutely forbids them. We are concerned with morality rather than with the status of such agreements in positive law.

The idea expressed by "cruelty and humiliation" is connected with another idea besides crimes against humanity: "cruel and unusual punishment." "Cruel and unusual punishment" is an amalgam of cruelty and humiliation. In my rendering of the expression, the regime is cruel *and* humiliating, and not merely cruel *or* humiliating, and that is what that amalgam is meant to convey. The historical examples of cruel and unusual punishment are indeed cases of crushing humiliation on top of horrific physical pain. The authors of the English Bill of Rights (1689), where the expression "cruel and unusual punishment" originated, much like the framers of the Eighth Amendment of the U.S. Constitution a hundred years later, were still familiar with the horrible punishment for treason: the victims were hanged, drawn, and quartered. What lies beyond this schematic formula is horrific reality. The victim was dragged on a wooden frame to the place of execution, hanged by the neck until almost dead, then disemboweled and emasculated, then beheaded, and finally split into four pieces. It is quite clear that the meaning of this extraordinary spectacle is to create an amalgam of cruelty and humiliation: attack on the integrity of the body both before and after death for the sole purpose of degradation. Hitler intended the same degradation in his punishment of those who had plotted against him in July 1944, claiming that they would be "hung like cattle." Not treating the dead body of the condemned as human dead body is an expression of humiliation.

All in all, there is an intimate relation between the notion of a regime of cruelty and humiliation and the two ideas of cruel and unusual punishment and of crime against humanity.

Here is a serious difficulty. Why not term as rotten any agreement with a gravely unjust regime? Why confine rottenness merely to cases of crimes against humanity? If grave injustice coincides with our sense of a regime of cruelty and humiliation, then there is no problem. But if gross injustice coincides with a regime of cruelty and humiliation, but then extends beyond it to cover, say, cases of gross injustice in the distribution of goods, what then?

Injustice may mean the absence of justice in the way unfriendliness may mean the absence of friendliness. But absence of friendliness can have a mild form, perhaps what most people feel in general. It may also, however, mean serious hostility and aggressiveness (as in "unfriendly fire"): something that most people feel some of the time and some people feel most of the time. Injustice in its gravest sense is comparable to unfriendliness in its hostile aggressive sense.

Grave injustice is bad, very bad. Why not term a compromise with a regime of grave injustice a rotten compromise? Such a declaration would have consequences. It means one should not make agreements that directly or indirectly associate the parties with a grave injustice, under any circumstances.

Grave injustice is a perfectly good reason not to engage with a wicked regime in signing a voluntary agreement that may help establish or maintain such a pattern. However, the question is: is it a good enough reason to prevent the signing of a peace agreement with such a regime under any circumstances? This is not an arbitrary example. It is the litmus test for what "under any circumstances" means. Crimes against humanity trump a peace agreement under any circumstances. But should injustice, not covered by my heading of a regime of cruelty and humiliation, trump any possible peace agreement?

Not in my book. Of course, we don't want to recognize injustice, especially not grave injustice. But what if the trade-off is peace for recognition of injustice? When this is the trade-off, there is no justification for not accepting injustice come what may, when what may come is war. The trade-off between peace and injustice should be dealt with on its merits, case by case. Only crimes against humanity, which I interpret as crimes against the possibility of morality, should trump peace in all circumstances and should never be recognized in a compromise.

-3-

COMPROMISING FOR PEACE

Road Map

KANT, IN HIS justly celebrated essay "Toward Lasting Peace," contrasted truce, as a suspension of hostilities, with lasting peace. His first article reads, "No treaty of peace shall be held valid in which there is tacitly reserved matter for future war."[1] Otherwise, he says, the treaty is only a truce.

I shall deal here with the territorial aspect of a peace agreement that might undermine lasting peace. It could be termed the *irredentism* clause or, more forcefully, the *revanchism* clause in a peace agreement. Irredentism is a foreign policy aiming at regaining lost territories; revanchism adds an element of revenge to such policy. "Irredentism" and "revanchism" are nineteenth-century terms that reappear in a modern nationalistic context. "Irredentism" was coined in Italy, "revanchism" in France, both referring to political campaigns aimed at regaining lost national territories. I use the term "irredentism" in a broader context by linking it to the religious picture of politics.

A party to a peace agreement has many reasons to break the agreement: it's too costly, too inconvenient. Irredentism is only one reason for breaking an agreement. Why worry about this particular sort of breach when agreements are breached for endless sorts of reasons? I am concerned about the lingering sense of injustice that might undermine the stability of peace. It is part and parcel of a general worry about the relation between peace and justice. Historically, irredentism had a great deal to do with the lingering sense of injustice felt by those who lost territories.

Justice, like linguistics, may be approached in two ways: historically or synchronically. Distributive justice—with the paradigm of dividing the cake justly—is synchronic, whereas the paradigm of who queued first serves the historical notion of justice.[2] A sense of injustice expressed in irredentism can be historical or it can be synchronic.

A historical sense of justice fits well the picture of politics as religion, whereas a synchronic sense of justice fits the economic view better.

There are two types of appeal to historical justice in irredentism.

Type one goes like this: We were there first. It once belonged to us. It was in our hands for many years. It was taken by force. At a moment of weakness, our ancestors acquiesced in an agreement that gave up the land, but that was inherently unjust. Our forefathers' unjust deal should be renegotiated. In a new deal, the land should return to us. We are its true historical owners.

Type two goes like this: The disputed land cries out to be redeemed. It was a constitutive element in our past and is a formative element in our current identity. We deserve this land because of its significance to the life of our people. It means nothing to those who now have power over it. For them, it is nothing but a piece of real estate, whereas for us it means everything.

These two claims accompany the justification for historical irredentism.

The distributive sense of injustice has a different nature. J. Paul Getty famously said something to the effect that he did not mind if the poor inherited the earth as long as he held the mineral rights.[3] Those who, because of the peace agreement, become poor in minerals resent those who end up with a great deal of such resources (e.g., oil and diamonds). This is a typical irredentism on distributive ground. These two irredentist claims may in practice blend inextricably together, but they can and should be conceptually separated.

I try to account for both kinds of irredentism. Yet my concern is not irredentism as such, but rather irredentism as a case that sheds light on the relation between peace and justice, with compromise in between.

In the first part of this chapter, I claim that the politics of the holy is strongly irredentist and as such threatens the idea of lasting peace. In the second part, I deal with the way we should morally do away with the unfinished business of (justified) irredentism, so as to make room for lasting peace.

The Holy and Irredentism

The religious idea of the holy sets severe limits on the ability of humans to negotiate and compromise. Holy places, holy days, holy artifacts—are all dedicated to God. I shall limit myself here to holy sites and territories because they are the locus of so much current political discussion. There is a paradox here. On the one hand, the whole universe is the domain of God; but on the other hand, the domain of God is limited to sacred grounds—all the rest is profane, the realm of what is humanly negotiable.

In the history of religion, three competing views exist on what makes something holy. One view is that a place is holy because humans consecrate and dedicate it to God. Another view is that humans consecrate a place because it is objectively holy: a divine presence was previously there, and this is why it is sanctified. In the Hebrew Bible, there is yet a third view of how a place becomes holy: when people first consecrate the place, which then receives a sign from God approving it.

In the actual practice of the three religions of Judaism, Christianity, and Islam, we find various combinations of these three views. When humans make a place holy by declaring it so, there is some room for negotiation. It appears that the believers may divest it of its holiness without desecrating it, yet as long as the place is declared holy, it is holy, and there is little room for negotiation. On all counts of the holy, the domain of the holy should be free from human manipulation and human interests. It is the domain of God, his sanctuary. Violating God's honor by compromising what is due to God alone is anathema, an act of worshipping evil.

The idea of the holy is not unique to monotheism. The politics of the holy when the dispute is between believers in one God (say, Jews and Muslims over the holiness of the Temple Mount) is as bitter as when the dispute is between monotheists and polytheists (say, Muslims and Hindus over the Babri Mosque in Ayodhya). There is, however, a belief that polytheistic religions allow much wider latitude for compromise and tolerance. This belief is conceptually plausible but factually doubtful.[4]

The politics of the holy is the art of the impossible. It makes long-run compromise untenable. If a site or a territory is considered holy, then a claim to it becomes an absolute claim.

When forced to make concessions, the believers view their concessions as a temporary setback. In their weakness, they may opt for truce but only for the sake of regaining strength, not for the sake of peace. The politics of the holy may include cessation of violence but never cessation of the expectation of violence. Thus the politics of the holy, I maintain, is inherently irredentist. Religious irredentism can be dormant and can erupt violently, but it cannot be discounted, even when dormant.

The believers regard themselves as the trustees of the holy and, as such, are not allowed to compromise at its expense. So if peace means both the cessation of violence and the cessation of the expectation of violence in the future, the politics of the holy is not the politics of peace based on compromise. Compromise is construed by the believers as an act of betrayal and not as a sensible way of splitting the difference.

The politics of the holy creates its own ideal advocates, the unbending ascetics who cannot be bought. Caesar was famously and superstitiously afraid of thin people, believing them dangerous and unyielding. But regimes are quite justified in being afraid of ascetic people who are not in the business of compromising and yet assume holy politics. Being crippled, say, like the Hamas leader Sheikh Yassin, or blind, like Sheikh Rahman, helps convey the impression that such men are political figures to whom nothing worldly can be offered in temptation. They may not and would not compromise their holy politics under any circumstances.

The claim about the uncompromising nature of the holy may be hedged significantly, especially with respect to holy sites. One hedge, typical of religions that have lost political and military power, is to spiritualize the holy—to remove the holy from the physical space. So if the Holy Sepulcher is held by Muslims, then Jerusalem is transposed by Christians into heavenly Jerusalem, the Jerusalem of the spirit rather than earthly Jerusalem, the Jerusalem of the flesh. But, as happened with the Crusaders, the nearer they approached Jerusalem, the more earthly the domain of God became to them. Retreat to the spiritual is one way in which the holy is negotiated within religion.

Another hedge is to rezone the holy, to retreat in space from the merely holy to the holy of holies, which includes placing the holy in the innermost citadel, the soul. Holy geography, like the geography of Paris, maps the world in concentric circles. The inner circle is the holy of holies: the further we move toward the outer circle, the further we move away from the holy. This structure of the holy space enables us, when the chips are down, to retreat to the inner circles and devalue the outer circles as if they didn't really count, or never really counted. In short, the holy is intricately structured, not simple and indivisible.

The Psychology of the Holy

The politics of the holy rarely occurs in history in undiluted form. When believers lack conviction, the holy becomes hollow. On the other hand, secular ideologies, especially nationalism, tend to acquire a taste for the politics of the holy. The fusion of nationalism and religion creates its own politics of the holy. The politics of the holy, whether in its pure religious form or as a fusion of religion and nationalism, is inherently hostile to any peace that implies compromising the honor of God. In the fusion of nationalism and religion, we find the following inference: if it is holy to me, it is mine. But in fact, the whole logic of the holy—if logic is the word—is that what is holy is neither yours nor mine; it is the domain of the divine.

Conversely, the holy as the negation of compromise can be viewed as a liberating idea that allows a wide range of compromises in matters that are not holy. The idea is that since the holy reduces the scope of nonnegotiable items to a very small list, what is not on the list is open to negotiation and compromise. People with fixed points in their lives should be and perhaps, in general, are more flexible than those who lack fixed points. Those without fixed points constantly vacillate between being unyielding and being flexible on each and every point. This is true, but it is also true that the adherents of the holy tend to resist compromise because they fear that by compromising, they are treading on a slippery slope. A compromise, any compromise, looks to the faithful like accepting the first premise in a slippery-slope argument: you accept A (the compromise), which clearly does not involve giving up on a fixed point, but then you are led by small steps to conclusion B, which *does* involve giving up on a fixed point, namely, an article of faith.

The issue here is not the logical validity of slippery-slope arguments. The issue is the psychological plausibility of the domino effect in moving from acceptance of A in a compromise to the sinful acceptance of B at the end of the day. The psychological assumption of many religions, as well as of many ideologies, is that with respect to strong views weakly held, the supporter of the faith should avoid accepting any premise that has slippery-slope potential. Between these two plausible, offsetting tendencies—fixed points increase overall flexibility and fixed points increase the fear of setting the believer on a treacherous slippery slope—it is hard to predict which tendency will prevail. All in all, I believe that the fear of compromise in general is less a fear of the specific compromise than it is a fear of taking the first step on a slippery slope. Compromise erodes integrity by imperceptible small steps, steps on a slippery slope.

Revolutionary Tactical Retreat

Revolutionary politics with regard to compromise, any compromise, is dominated by the religious picture. Revolutionary ideology views compromise as a lethal step on a very slippery slope that ends in selling out the revolutionary goals. Compromise with the enemies of the revolution diminishes the intensity of the revolutionary goal; an unclear goal is already corrupt. The term "rotten compromise" originated, I suspect, in the circles of revolutionary socialism.[5] Revisionists, Fabians, and social democrats are all versions of those who diminish the spirit of the revolution, in the sense of betraying it through their willingness to compromise with the exploiters.

Yet revolutionaries must sometimes compromise. They call it "historical necessity." Lenin, to save the Soviet Union from famine, had to compromise with the peasantry by allowing a free market in agricultural products. The concession of large chunks of Russia to Germany in the Treaty of Brest-Litovsk (ratified in 1918) is another glaring example of historical necessity. But such compromises should be judged as unavoidable necessities, depending on who signs on behalf of the workers, not on what is signed.

Revolutionary compromise is rotten and hence not excusable through an appeal to historical necessity, if the one signing it cannot be trusted to protect the interests of the working class. Lenin, we were told by the Bolsheviks, was allowed to compromise, for we could rest assured that he merely engaged in a tactical retreat for the sake of saving the revolution, but never in a strategic ("historical") compromise. Compromise as historical necessity is not a historical compromise: it is only a truce, never peace.

During the 1970s, Enrico Berlinguer, then secretary of the Communist Party in Italy, advanced the notion of *historical compromise* (*compromesso storico*): the idea of joining forces with the conservative Christian Democrats to help stabilize the political and economic situation in Italy. It was clear that the expression "historical compromise" meant not a temporary truce in the class struggle, but a total reorientation and accommodation with the existing order.

Conceptually, there is no place for historical compromise in a revolutionary ideology. If the compromise is historical rather than a mere temporary necessity of tactical retreat, what is compromised is the very idea of the revolution.

Compromise as Truce

The holy feeds politics with the idea that compromise is never peace but only truce. The dialectic among truce, peace, and the holy is exemplified in the pact of Hudaybiyya, which sheds light, or cast its shadow, on political Islam today. In 628 AD, Muhammad arranged for a pilgrimage to the Q'aba in Mecca. The Quraysh tribe that controlled Mecca at that time forbade him to advance toward Mecca. A negotiation took place in Hudaybiyya, resulting in an insulting treaty. Muhammad was to turn back anyone who came to his camp without the permission of his guardians, but anyone from Muhammad's camp who defected to the Quraysh was not to be sent back. Muhammad was harshly criticized by his most devoted supporters. "Aren't you truly the Apostle of Allah?"

The Prophet said, "Yes, indeed." "Isn't our cause just and the cause of the enemy unjust?" He said, "Yes." "Then why should we be humble in our religion?"[6] Later Muhammad broke the treaty of Hudaybiyya. He refused to hand over women who had joined him and whose guardians requested that he send them back, and was willing only to restore their dowries.

The story of the treaty of Hudaybiyya is of great significance for an understanding of the politics of the holy and the possibility of compromise therein. The Hudaybiyya treaty was a temporary peace agreement with the idolatrous, and hence a temporary retreat in an all-out war against idolatry. To reach a compromise with the idolatrous on matters that pertain to the holy is to compromise the holy. Making a pilgrimage to the Q'aba is clearly an issue that pertains to the holy. Handing back people who have joined your religion, thus returning them to idolatrous practices, is another. At stake at Hudaybiyya were not worldly matters such as returning stray camels, but serious matters that affected the foundations of the Messenger's faith.

The elements of the Hudaybiyya treaty are as follows: the Messenger of God is not recognized as such by those who stop him on the way. His loyalists take this as an affront to the Prophet and a mortification of their religion. This act of mortification justifies a war or at least avoidance of the pilgrimage to Q'aba. It does not allow for compromise: the agreement is not an outcome of coercion. The sole justification of the agreement is its temporary status, limited in time, with no real commitment to abide by it, should circumstances allow otherwise.

If this is the right reading of the story, then it implies that there is no room for a genuine peace treaty but only for a limited truce between the emissaries of the holy, who act in the name of God, and the infidels. I hasten to add that this is not peculiar to Islam: Judaism and Christianity can provide similar instances. When it comes to the holy, then, compromise is truce and not peace. Is that the case with morality, too, so that compromise on what is just is a truce and not permanent peace?

Justification of Peace

As I said in the introduction, although political philosophers have dealt with the notion of lasting (permanent) peace, they hardly, if ever, have dealt with the notion of just peace. The claim is that peace does not need justification: whenever war is unjustified, peace is by that very fact justified. There is a very strong presumption in favor of peace, for the obvious reason that peace is the negation of large-scale violence: it is the use of violence that calls for justification, not its absence. So the presumption of peace can be opposed only by strong reasons to renounce it. Not every case of injustice justifies opposing the presumption of peace, for violence is bad, very bad.

Frances Kamm, in her extremely illuminating account, deals "at a very general level" with a thesis we both share: some injustices must be tolerated to prevent the resort to war.[7] Peace, any peace, is justified as long as the presumption of peace is not opposed, that is, where war cannot justly alter a relevant state of peace. The burden of proof is on whoever advocates war. A *justification* to deviate from peace does not mean an *obligation* to deviate. It means only, as Kamm rightly observes, *permission*, not obligation, whereas the presumption in favor of peace prescribes an obligation to keep peace unless and until it is opposed. However, in rare cases, the moral presumption is reversed in favor of war, and the burden of proof is on those who do not advocate war. This is the case where the very idea of morality is challenged, as in the case of Hitlerism. In such cases, the countries that remain neutral should justify their stand. It is indeed because of such extreme cases—cases in which the very presumption of peace is reversed, so that one has to justify why one is not at war—that we should not view the theory of just peace as the mere flip side of the theory of just war.

So far two states of affairs have been mentioned: war and peace, peace being the cessation of war, war being the collapse of peace. But there is a third state of affairs, truce, a mere temporary peace. My concern is with the relation between truce and permanent peace: when does compromise allow us—morally, that is—to turn truce into peace, and when does it not?

The politics of the holy provides us with the idea that when it comes to negotiating on matters holy, only a temporary peace is acceptable. One may think that the relation between peace and justice should be shaped on the model of the relation between peace and the holy. Conflict over the holy, like conflict over justice, enables at most a state of *truce* but never an acceptance of *permanent peace*. Truce with respect to the holy (read *justice*) is not rotten, but permanent peace is. On the model of the holy, peace is incompatible with the acceptance of injustice. Temporary peace can suffer injustice, but permanent peace should not.

Another approach to peace says that peace should tolerate a certain injustice as long as the injustice can realistically be remedied by nonviolent means. There is no justification for redressing any form of injustice by war: only very serious cases of injustice offer a justification to wage war, provided the remaining injustices—which do not justify war—can realistically be remedied by nonviolent means. War might on occasion be the most efficient and speedy way to redress injustice, but this in itself does not justify its use.

My view on the relation between peace and justice is different from the ones just expressed. In my view, for the sake of lasting peace, it is justifiable to accept permanently some injustices, the removal of which is not meant to be pursued by violence, but which nevertheless carry the potential to deteriorate into war. Irredentism has this potential.

Kamm's concern is confined to making war and ending war; I am also concerned with ending war in ways that will not leave room for resuming it later on. It is in transforming truce into peace that we may be required to trade justice for peace. Let me switch my philosophical documentary style of commenting on real past and present events in favor of a more stylized thought experiment. This thought experiment is in some ways a fleshing out of Frances Kamm's austere schematic account. On the whole, I have little trust in stylized examples in philosophy, so I tried to make the following stylized examples as close to real cases as I could.

When Peace Trumps Justice

Over a generation ago, the predator state Over-Dog attacked, without any moral justification, the state Under-Dog. Over-Dog conquered two provinces of Under-Dog: Bread and Butter. It has retained the two provinces ever since. The conquered province of Bread is heavily populated by Under-Dog people, whereas province Butter is an arid land with a thinly spread population. The densely populated province Bread is subjected to a very harsh military rule that amounts to trampling grossly on the human rights of the Under-Dog people there.

The most important event in Under-Dog history occurred many years ago in province Butter. It was the famous Battle of the Eagles. Province Butter also contains the most important historical site of the Under-Dog people: a cemetery and shrine for those who fell in that battle. In the collective memory of Under-Dog, no event looms as important as the Battle of the Eagles. Ever since the occupation, Under-Dog people have had no access to the cemetery and have been unable to commemorate the battle, as they had been doing for years and years, while it was still theirs. In addition, some promising signs of natural gas with serious commercial potential have recently been discovered in province Butter.

These two spaces, province Bread and province Butter, express different time orientations: province Butter is oriented toward the past (the Battle of the Eagles) and the future (the promise of gas); province Bread is oriented toward the present (the currently depressing state of its oppressed population).

Let us assume that Under-Dog is justified in waging a war only on account of the population of Bread. Under-Dog is not justified in going to war on account of Butter, even though justice requires that province Butter—as well as Bread— should be returned to Under-Dog.

Let us also assume that the condition for compromise in the form of the possibility of regaining it all holds in the following way: if Under-Dog does its military best and Over-Dog does its worst, then Under-Dog has a chance of regaining the lost provinces. If, on the other hand, Over-Dog performs only indifferently, it can cling to Bread and Butter, no matter how well Under-Dog performs. Yet Bread and Butter mean much more to the Under-Dogs than to the Over-Dogs. Moreover, Under-Dog has a tremendous nuisance value to Over-Dog; it can, for example, acutely embarrass Over-Dog in world opinion. To avoid a winnable yet costly war and preempt Under-Dog's nuisance value, Over-Dog is willing to offer a compromise. Here are various scenarios of compromises that Over-Dog might offer Under-Dog, and their implications.

Scenario 1

Take either Bread or Butter but not both. Whatever you choose, you should effectively forfeit your claim to the alternative not taken. You are not entitled to nourish any expression of irredentism with regard to Bread or to Butter. You should, for example, remove from your school textbooks any explicit or implicit claims to the forsaken province. Giving up on your irredentism is for us Over-Dogs the only measure of good faith in concluding a permanent peace that is not a mere truce.

Suppose that Under-Dog goes for the suggested compromise and chooses Bread. It must then waive its claim to Butter and refrain from pursuing any move to regain Butter, including pursuit by nonviolent means. This is tough. The demand to waive a just claim is unjust. Yet what is the force of Under-Dog's promise to refrain in the future from pursuing its claims to the lost province?

One response is that the force of the promise is very limited. On the one hand, it is bad to break a promise; on the other hand, it is bad not to get back what belongs to you in justice. Under-Dog has to weigh what is worse: breaking its promise or breaking with its heritage. Under-Dog should opt for the lesser evil: breaking a promise to a bully seems, on the face of it, considerably less evil than giving up for good what justly belongs to you. By this line of thought, justice trumps peace, and you are morally justified in accepting compromise as temporary peace, knowing that it is morally right to walk out on your promise.

A compromise of the kind suggested by Over-Dog should be regarded by Under-Dog as a shabby compromise, a compromise one may be allowed to accept tactically only to renounce it later on. Over-Dog is not morally entitled to expect that acceptance of its offered compromise is going to last and thus yield a permanent peace.

Note that Under-Dog's justification in breaking its promise does not mean that Under-Dog is morally justified in going to war over Butter: remember, Butter alone does not justify going to war. So what does breaking the promise to renounce irredentism amount to? It means that Under-Dog is justified in effectively pursuing and diligently regaining the lost province by any means at its disposal short of war: for example, by lobbying hard to impose international economic sanctions on Over-Dog. I suppose that this fits Kamm's position.

My response is different. The promise to give up on an irredentist claim has a specially moral force, much beyond the ordinary moral force of keeping one's promises. It is a promise for the sake of permanent peace. This worthy cause endows the promise with a special binding force: we do not want to live in a world where a peace agreement is no more than a ceasefire; we want a peace agreement to be more binding than other normal agreements because of our immense stake in peace. Signing an agreement for the sake of peace, even if it includes unjust terms, has a strong binding force not just on those who sign it but on future generations. A shabby compromise like the one suggested by Over-Dog, if signed, should be respected.

Scenario 2

As before, Over-Dog offers Under-Dog Bread or Butter but not both. Unlike the previous case, Under-Dog opts for the arid land with its glorious past and rosy future of gas, forgoing the liberation of its oppressed people who are constantly humiliated and treated cruelly. This is a rotten compromise. Under-Dog should not sign such an agreement. In a peculiar way, it is the Under-Dogs who make it rotten: they could have opted for the shabby agreement of the previous scenario. It is rotten because it recognizes and helps maintain a state of affairs based on cruelty and humiliation. It is a compromise that should not see the light of day. But if it does, is the next generation of Under-Dog free to revoke the agreement, declare it rotten, and regain its moral justification to go to war on behalf of Bread? My answer is no.

In opting for Butter when Bread was offered, Under-Dog lost its justification to go to war later. It may be the case that the situation in province Bread is so wretched that outside intervention on behalf of Bread is justified on the grounds of human rights, but Under-Dog has no special moral standing in the matter; it lost it by signing a rotten compromise.

Scenario 3

Over-Dog offers Under-Dog province Butter, on condition that all irredentist activity with regard to province Bread should end immediately. Remember, it is Bread that justifies Under-Dog's going to war, but here Bread is not on offer. In light of that fact, how morally different for Under-Dog is this scenario from the previous one, in which Bread was offered? What is the binding force of Under-Dog's promise in the co-promise to forfeit any claim to Bread in the future? Let me review two responses.

First response: extract from the aggressor whatever you can without war, namely, in this case, Butter. Wait for an opportunity to walk out on your promise and keep trying to regain Bread, by war if necessary. You are not in the wrong if you break your promise to an aggressor who oppresses your people. The prospect of exploiting the gas of Butter in the future is a very good reason for Under-Dog to accept what is offered, since among other things it enhances its chance to regain Bread by war.

Second response: the right thing to do, from a moral point of view, is to reject Over-Dog's offer outright and retain an unimpeachable right to wage war over Bread. If, however, you go for the shabby compromise (shabby and not rotten since Bread was not on offer), then you should keep your promise to give Bread up entirely for the sake of peace: this is true, provided that the agreement includes the elimination of cruelty and humiliation for your people in Bread. If you cannot eliminate humiliation and cruelty, don't sign, because then it is clearly a rotten compromise.

We can go on and toy with more elaborate combinations, but the general drift should be clear by now. We are facing two conflicting intuitions: in one, peace based on compromise is justified, even if only partial justice is granted, as long as Under-Dog retains the right and the might to struggle for the remaining justice and has a fair chance of achieving it.

In another intuition, my own, peace based on compromise is justified even if, for its sake, Under-Dog has to give up war, or even a nonviolent struggle, for that cause. This is justified because it removes rational fears of future violent irredentism. It is the sacrifice of some justice for the cause of peace. This second intuition pits peace against justice in a radical way. It is willing to put up with partial injustice for good, provided that it is done for the sake of permanent peace. This is a true clash of peace and justice.

Justice and Stability

An immensely important treatise about peace is Keynes's *The Economic Consequences of the Peace* (1920), written in the very specific context of the Versailles peace treaty. In writing this passage, Keynes was thinking both about peace and about justice. "The task of the peace conference is to honor engagements and to satisfy justice: *but no less* to re-establish life and to heal wounds" (emphasis added).[8] The way I read Keynes, the "but no less" phrase ought to be replaced by "but even more." Keynes was predominantly interested in the stability of peace. Carthaginian peace[9] in Europe would not only be unjust; it would, more importantly, be unstable. The issue I raise is this: what price should we pay in terms of justice for the sake of a stable peace? The stability of peace seems to be an empirical question, and indeed it is. But it should also concern pure normative theory.

Let us go back to our little thought experiment. It assumes that Over-Dog is barely interested in justice as such but recognizes that a strong sense of injustice on the part of the victim has a motivating force to destabilize its conquest. So Over-Dog is willing to offer the minimum justice required to deflect the prospect of war. It wants to retain not simply the absolute maximum of conquest but the maximum of conquest compatible with long-run stability. Over-Dog, out of prudence, has a keen interest not in truce but in permanent peace: a recognized permanent peace serves its long-run interests best. Under-Dog knows that its best bet is to gain the moral high ground, since world sympathy for its cause is the best weapon it has against Over-Dog. We may say that Under-Dog's side, for whatever reason, cares more about morality, even if not for its own sake.

In any case the perspective we have addressed so far with regard to the normative relation between peace and justice is the perspective of Under-Dog. The question I keep asking is this: what should Under-Dogs sacrifice for the sake of permanent peace? Directing the question to the Under-Dogs seems grossly unfair. It is unfair to make moral demands on only the victims, instead of addressing the question of what one should do to the predators for the sake of peace. Why not ask the Over-Dogs what they should sacrifice for peace? The reason I did not address the perspective of the Over-Dogs is that it is uninteresting. The moral demand on Over-Dog is clear and distinct: for the sake of peace and for the sake of justice Over-Dog should give back Bread and Butter to Under-Dog, period. This is so clear and so boringly right that there is nothing useful to add to it.

The moral demand on Under-Dog, however, is less clear and less distinct, and hence more interesting: in facing Over-Dog you are justified in going to war to regain Bread and Butter. If offered Bread (the morally justifying reason for war), with an option of regaining Butter by nonviolent means later, you should not wage war. If offered Bread, but on condition that you give up any struggle, violent or not, for Butter, you may morally reject the offer, even though your moral justification to go to war is only over Bread and not over Butter. But if you accept in its entirety the terms of the Butter-for-Bread compromise, the compromise is morally binding: it is binding because it is done for a very good cause—for the cause of peace. Peace, unlike war, deserves a great deal of sacrifice.

- 4 -

Compromise and Political Necessity

The Problem

A ROTTEN COMPROMISE is an agreement to establish or
maintain a regime of cruelty and humiliation—in short, an
inhuman regime, in the literal sense of inhuman, unfit for
humans. Regime has two meanings: one refers to government, the other to a regular pattern of behavior. A rotten
compromise has predominantly to do with a pattern of rotten behavior, and only derivatively to do with the government responsible for creating such a pattern.

Not every compromise with a rotten regime is rotten. A
compromise is rotten only if it establishes or maintains an inhuman regime. The "or" is nonexclusive; an agreement might
do both: establish and maintain. However, if an agreement
with an inhuman regime neither establishes nor helps maintain the regime, the agreement is not rotten.

North Korea is an inhuman regime. But it may very well
be the case that trade agreements with North Korea weaken
in the long run the hold of the regime, whereas embargo and
isolation help maintain it and make it even more inhuman.

One may think that a rotten regime is the best to judge
what helps it. If the regime wants the agreement, it is a sure

sign that it helps maintain it. It ain't necessarily so. A regime may seek an agreement that solves a short-run pressing problem, whereas in the long run the agreement undermines its hold. Note that the long run should not exceed the life span of the desert generation.

In the case of the Nazi regime, I made an exception by making the government the predominant carrier of rottenness, since that government was dedicated to the promotion of *radical* evil. In its far-reaching racism, it denied the idea of shared humanity, and thereby undermined the very idea of morality. However, even in the case of Nazi Germany, not every possible agreement with its rulers was rotten in and of itself. I have already mentioned that on April 25, 1944, Adolf Eichmann, on behalf of the upper command of the SS, offered a deal known as "Blood for Trucks," the gist of which was exchanging one million Jews for ten thousand trucks. That is, the Jews of Hungary could leave, and thus be saved, in exchange for the Allies' ensuring that Nazi Germany got trucks. The Allies turned down the offer, with good reasons, but moral rottenness was not one of them. Had the deal been accepted, it would have saved many people from humiliation and destruction.

I accompanied the expression "rotten compromise" with an emphatic clause: a rotten compromise is an agreement that should be avoided, *come what may*. But aren't there some circumstances that override the "come what may" clause, circumstances that compel us to tolerate rotten compromises? We may cogently think that a plea of necessity, perhaps similar to the one by which we justify self-defense, may justify signing a rotten compromise. If so, then, what necessity, if any, could *justify* concluding a rotten compromise?

My answer, dogmatically put, is: nothing. But then we may ask a different question: can "political necessity" *excuse* rather than *justify* concluding a rotten compromise? Justification serves as a plea for authorization ahead of the deed. Excuses serve as a plea for forgiveness after the deed. In the case of excuses we basically say: We did it. It is really bad, but there was no alternative. We did what we did out of necessity. You must forgive us or at least understand us. (After all, you wouldn't have acted differently, had you been in our place.)

Two clarifications concerning my use of "political necessity" are in order. In adding "political" to qualify "necessity," we refer to collective decisions or to decisions on behalf of a collective, rather than to individual decisions concerning private matters. By "necessity" I mean not metaphysical necessity but rather a situation in which no reasonable alternative is left. A lack of reasonable alternatives does not preclude unreasonable alternatives, which, although unreasonable, are nevertheless ontological possibilities. Thus, for example, in every situation of a choice between doing one thing or doing another, there is almost always a "shadow" possibility of committing collective suicide, thereby avoiding the need to choose between the two. But collective suicide can hardly be regarded as a reasonable alternative. Collective suicide is an ontological possibility, but only rarely is it also a political possibility.

Necessity and Coercion

Necessity—being left with no reasonable alternatives—comes close to one important sense of coercion: coercion as a condition in which, being left with no reasonable alternatives, we do, against our better judgment, what others want us to do. The intimate relation between coercion and political necessity brings up a difficulty, since an agreement based on coercion is not a compromise. Being forced to agree with an inhuman regime is not a compromise, and by the very same act not a rotten compromise. So using necessity to justify or to excuse can neither justify nor excuse, for necessity means coercion and coercion undermines the idea of compromise.

Leaping from necessity to coercion and from coercion to no-compromise and from no-compromise to no-rotten-compromise is just too facile. It does not release us from the need to sort out the relation between compromise and necessity. To do so, we need a distinction and a perspective. Here is the distinction: a rotten compromise has an *active* side and a *passive* side. The active side is the side that inflicts cruelty and humiliation, whereas the passive side is the side that agrees to it. For simplicity, I shall assume only two sides to a compromise.

There are two types of passive sides: a *silent partner* and a *sleeping partner.* A silent partner does not in fact inflict the inhuman regime of cruelty and humiliation, but helps bring it about, first by signing the agreement, and then by helping to implement it. For example, a silent partner might hand over the victims and leave it to the active side to treat the victims inhumanly. By contrast, a sleeping partner does not actively participate in anything beyond signing the rotten agreement.

As for the sleeping partner, we should distinguish between a partner whose signature is a necessary condition for establishing a rotten regime and one that in signing a rotten compromise helps the active side, but without its contribution being vital to the active partner's policy. For example, it helps the active partner gain legitimacy, but the active partner would have installed the rotten regime with or without the consent of the passive partner.

There is, however, a further distinction between an active partner and a passive one. We have heard reports of cases of extraordinary rendition agreements whereby the CIA kidnapped and transferred more than one hundred suspects to other countries (mainly Egypt, but also Syria, Morocco, Jordan, and Uzbekistan) for interrogation. According to those reports, "torture by proxy" was used systematically. If this is true, we should regard the United States not as a silent partner in such rendition agreements, but as an active one, in spite of the fact that the infliction of torture, cruelty, and humiliation was outsourced. The instigator, the United States, and the subcontractors should both be considered an active side.

The distinction between an active side and a passive side does not tell us who benefits from the wrong perpetrated. For example, the active side in perpetrating the apartheid policy in South Africa consisted of a relatively small number of whites, but the number of white sleeping partners who benefited and supported the apartheid policy was large. In contrast, the number of active perpetrators in Rwanda's genocide of the Hutu was large, but the number that benefited from it was very small.[1]

I could add more and more epicycles to the distinction between passive and active partners, some of them quite useful, but for simplicity's sake, I shall rely mostly on the crude distinction between an active side and a passive side to a rotten compromise. The active side is rotten for what it does (cruelty and humiliation), the passive side for what it agrees can be done in its name.

I adopt the perspective of the passive partner. It is a better perspective from which to discuss the moral status of a rotten compromise. It tells us what is wrong with a rotten compromise as such, namely, as an *agreement* to a regime of cruelty and humiliation, without conflating it with the *perpetration* of cruelty and humiliation by the active side.

The purest and toughest case for us to tackle is the categorical injunction "Thou shall not sign a rotten compromise, come what may," when directed at a sleeping partner. It is tough because the consent of the sleeping partner is not supposed to make any difference in terms of installing the regime of cruelty and humiliation. Yet the sleeping partner is asked to refrain from signing such an agreement, and to bear whatever consequences such avoidance might incur.

Equipped with the distinction between active and passive partners in a rotten compromise, let us go back to the issue of the relation between necessity and coercion. Compromise is a noncoercive agreement. So by definition the passive side to a rotten compromise is not coerced by the active side. Yet the passive side may face a situation perilously close to coercion. Let me present the situation first in schematic format, then in a meaty historical example.

A is in a war to the death with B. A believes that it desperately needs C's help to counter B. C is a menacing regime. C offers to help A, if and only if A hands D over to C. C would suppress D by subjugating it to a regime of cruelty and humiliation. A knows full well what awaits poor D at the hands of C. C does not coerce A to accept its rotten offer, but the situation of war with B makes A realize that it has no alternative but to accept a rotten compromise with C.

In my view, C exploits the vulnerability of A, but it does not coerce A to accept the rotten agreement. The reason is that in offering the option of becoming A's ally, C does not make A's situation any worse than it was before the rotten offer was made. The fact that C does not worsen the relative situation of A means that C does not, at least technically, coerce A, but it comes pretty close to coercion when A believes that it has no reasonable alternative but to accept a rotten compromise and hand D over to A for inhuman treatment.

A Meaty Example

The formative example for my discussion of the relation between political necessity and rotten compromise is the Yalta agreement (of February 1945). I am going to divide the Yalta agreement into two parts, using the agreement as two formative examples. The first part has to do with the forced repatriation of Soviet soldiers and citizens to the Soviet Union. The second part is the agreement to suppressive Soviet rule over Central and Eastern Europe.

One may protest by saying that the wording of the Yalta agreement says nothing about forced repatriation or any kind of suppression. On the contrary, Stalin committed himself in Yalta to an article that says that "the liberated peoples could freely choose their form of government."[2] Similarly, the Yalta agreement mentions repatriation, but not forced repatriation. One may conclude, wrongly, I believe, that these two events, the forced repatriation and the subjugation of Eastern and Central Europe, were in fact violations of the agreement. This may be technically true, but it was quite clear to both sides what "the deal" was beyond the wording of the agreement. "The deal" was rotten on both counts: forced repatriation and de facto recognition of Stalin's rule over Central and Eastern Europe.

My interest is more in "the deal" than in the wording of the Yalta agreement. I am less interested in the Yalta agreement in the technical sense of the term, although wording plays a role in the assessment of a deal's rottenness. The first part, repatriation, is a deal between an active partner, the Soviet Union, and a silent partner, the Western Allies. The second part, which deals with Soviet rule in Eastern and Central Europe, is between an active partner, the Soviet Union, and a sleepy partner, the Western Allies. We should probe whether the distinction between a silent and a sleepy partner to a rotten agreement carries moral weight.

Since I am dealing with a meaty example, let me repeat a point I have already made: I have good reasons to turn to the Second World War as a source of seminal examples. The Second World War is to morality what the supercollider is to physics: extreme moral experiences and observations emerged out of the high-energy clashes. The Second World War engaged both combatants and civilians in massive ways. In the bloody First World War, only 10 percent of the casualties of the war were civilians; in the Second World War, that figure rose to 50 percent. The Second World War was indeed a world war. In the Second World War humanity at large was involved. It is thus a fertile field to test the extreme circumstances of war (the extent to which civilians were involved) and the sense of shared humanity in a war that involved humanity at large.

A world war is an ordeal by fire for the idea of shared humanity, an idea on which morality is based. The practitioners of just-war theory take very few wars as clear cases of a just war. The war of the Allies against Nazi Germany is one of the few clear cases. By "just," I mean the just entry into war (*jus ad bellum*), rather than the just conduct of war (*jus in bello*) or the just settlement of war (*jus post bellum*). The Yalta conference took place during the war, but it dealt mainly with the end of the war.

The intense involvement and struggle with evil in the war invites us to view some of the choices in the war as tragic, in the Greek understanding of "tragic" as pertaining to matters of evil and necessity. So it is natural to ask whether necessary rotten compromises related to the war were tragic choices.[3] We do not intend to cast Churchill in the role of a tragic hero; he was too boisterous and too triumphant. Moreover, he never looked like someone checkmated by fate; rather, he looked like someone who cornered fate. Churchill made some noble choices: facing Germany alone after the collapse of France was perhaps his finest hour. But he also made some rotten choices: the indiscriminate aerial bombardment of German cities that killed hundreds of thousands of civilians was perhaps the most rotten of all. Churchill was a hero, even if by temperament he was not a tragic hero, and we owe him a great deal. He made the moral universe safe for free discussion. We also owe him a closer look at the Yalta agreement to see whether it was a rotten compromise based on a tragic choice, or whether it was rotten to the core.

The best soup is totally spoiled by even one cockroach.[4] It's not any good to say that the soup is delicious, and to ignore the cockroach. Do compromises follow the logic of the cockroach in the soup, such that a compromise is forever spoiled by one rotten clause? Or do compromises instead follow the logic of the fly in the ointment, whereby a rotten clause in a compromise makes it a flawed compromise, but not so completely as to qualify it as rotten?

Let us compare two agreements: an *ointment agreement* and a *cockroach agreement*, Versailles and Yalta. The treaty of Versailles that formally ended the First World War was not so much a compromise between the Allies and Germany as a compromise between the United States and the Allies in Europe, with regard to the issue of what terms to impose on Germany.

The French advocated harsh terms, the Americans relatively lenient terms, and the British were in between. There is no question that Clemenceau, representing France, advocated punitive terms meant not only to take territorial revenge, but to humiliate Germany as well. The war guilt clause (Article 231), which required Germany to accept sole responsibility for the war and make good all damages done to the civilian populations of the Allies, was an expression of Clemenceau's attitude that found a place in the treaty.[5]

But national humiliation, such as the humiliation of Germany in the treaty of Versailles, is not the kind of humiliation that renders a treaty rotten. The treaty did not create a regime in which the Germans were treated as nonhumans—the rotten sense of humiliation. It treated Germany as a defeated and disgraced nation, but not as a community of degraded human beings. The war guilt clause is, in my view, a fly in the ointment. It makes the treaty flawed, but it does not morally disqualify the treaty as a whole, whereas humiliation in the strong sense of human degradation differs from mere social humiliation in being a cockroach in the soup and not just a fly in the ointment. A rotten clause that excludes human beings from the human domain undermines the moral status of an agreement, for humiliation in the strong sense vitiates morality itself.

In contrast to Versailles, the Yalta agreement, together with the Tehran and Potsdam agreements, accepted the systematically cruel and humiliating rule of Stalin over Eastern Europe. It accepted a rule of human humiliation as opposed to mere social humiliation. It thereby rendered the Yalta agreement rotten.

Does it matter morally whether a rotten compromise is concluded for the sake of a just war or for the sake of peace? The Yalta agreement is ideal for testing this vexed question because it has the makings of both war and peace. The agreement was concluded during the war partly to sustain, until total victory, a just war against Nazi Germany, but it was also concluded with an eye to future peace in postwar Europe.

Historical examples are messy. But they are an important reality check for political morality. As a reality check, historical examples are preferable to stylized invented examples of the kind used in philosophical thought experiments. A reality check is particularly important when arguments of necessity are invoked to offset moral imperatives.

The idea is that we can always conjure imagined situations with such horrendous consequences that our most ingrained moral imperatives are overwhelmed to the point that we would be willing to give up any moral injunction just to prevent the horror awaiting us. The cliché has it that hard cases make for bad laws. Invented cases make for even worse laws.[6]

Operation Keelhaul

Operation Keelhaul is a code name for an operation conducted by American military forces in May and June of 1945. In its narrow sense, it consisted of the forcible handing over of Soviet war refugees in Austria to the Soviets. In its broad sense, however, it is a name for the total forced repatriation of Soviet prisoners of war and civilians to the Soviet Union. Julius Epstein writes, "'Operation Keelhaul' is the code designation that the U.S. Army gave to its own—top secret— documentary record of the forced repatriation of at least two million prisoners of war and displaced persons to Stalin's hangmen and slave labor camps."[7]

The code name "Keelhaul" is highly suggestive. The term comes from the wicked practice of punishment once used in the British and Dutch navies whereby the victim was hauled by ropes under the ship, with not much chance of survival. Calling the operation "Keelhaul" strongly suggests that those who planned the operation knew what lay in store for the poor victims. Alexander Solzhenitsyn called it "the last secret of the Second World War," and Nicholas Bethell named his most level-headed book on that subject *The Last Secret*. According to Solzhenitsyn and Bethell, its having been kept "top secret" long after all other secrets of the war had been revealed attests to the fact that the forced repatriation was so shameful that both Britain and the United States found it necessary to conceal it for as long as they could.[8]

Well, both Solzhenitsyn and Bethell were wrong about its being the last secret. It was not much of a secret. George Orwell, with his unfailing moral radar, had already recorded in 1946 the story of the sordid repatriation, though without many of the details that came to light only later. What is true, however, is not that it was the last secret, but that it was, perhaps, the last thing that the Western Allies publicly admitted, since they found it terribly embarrassing, something to be truly ashamed of.[9]

The Yalta agreement makes no mention of the use of force in the mutual repatriation. Yet there is no question that all sides to the Yalta agreement—accompanied by two bilateral agreements between the United States and the USSR and one between the United Kingdom and the USSR—had already agreed in Yalta that all prisoners of war and civilians would be repatriated, with or without their consent. Moreover, the Allies were under no illusions about what the forced repatriation implied. The obvious question, then, is this: was the Yalta agreement a rotten compromise, for no other reason than that it handed human beings over to systematic cruelty and humiliation?

For Alexander Solzhenitsyn, this is a rhetorical question that he compounds with his own query as to what military and political reason there can have been for the delivery to death at Stalin's hands of these hundreds of thousands of Soviet citizens.[10] (As a matter of fact, some of those forcibly sent back were not even Soviet soldiers or citizens; they were the descendants of the defeated counterrevolutionary Cossacks, who had already fled the Soviet Union after the First World War.)

For Hugh Trevor-Roper, however, the question is not rhetorical but tragic, a question of choosing between political necessity and morality. He is very aware of the tendency to conflate necessity and morality: "In the context of the time, perhaps they were judged moral. For men are not satisfied with necessity: they must justify it with morality—sometimes with a false morality which may outlast the real necessity." He goes on to explain: "The real *necessity,* in this story, was the alliance between Soviet Russia and the West which alone, after the mistakes of both partners in the 1930s, could defeat Germany and destroy Nazism."[11]

Trevor-Roper is keen to stress that necessity should be judged in the context of the time, and not in hindsight. Knowing how the war ended might cause us to think that there was no necessity for the forced repatriation. But for Trevor-Roper, how things look now is not relevant: the crucial question is how things looked then. I, however, think that the crucial question is different: how, *on reflection*, might things have looked at the time, if indeed there had been time to reflect? The hedge "on reflection" is a hedge against moral laziness. An appeal to necessity is justified only if hard thinking took place "at the time." Judging things by how they looked at the time, with no further qualifications, can serve as an invitation to moral laziness. Moral laziness is never a good excuse.

John Galsworthy, an involved official of the British Foreign Office, wrote at the time: "As far as I know, the basis of our interpretation is one of expediency. It would seem incongruous to expose the Anglo-Soviet relations to any further strain for the benefit of persons who have been active against our 'Ally.' This is not of course, the whole story: some of the people whom we are obliged to hand over are persons who have suffered under the Soviet regime for no fault of their own, have not fought against it, and are merely trying to escape it."[12]

An appeal to *expediency* is different from an appeal to *necessity*. Expediency is self-serving; it means whatever fits the agent's purpose at hand, especially if the purpose is an urgent need. In necessity, the purpose at hand has to do with survival. The means to that end should be the only reasonable ones to employ. Expediency suggests advantage, rather than moral correctness. Expediency is contrasted with principled behavior: politicians tend to present expediency as necessity, so as to give expediency a moral halo. Necessity deals with vital interests, in the strong sense of vital, namely, essential for continued existence. Expediency deals predominantly with interests pertinent to the effective conduct of the agent, not to its existence. Necessity has to do with the very existence of the agent, expediency merely with its well-being. "Expediency" and "necessity" both convey a sense of urgency, but whereas necessity conveys the idea that there are no alternatives, expediency does not.

Given the distinction between necessity and expediency, we should address two questions. Can political necessity trump morality and thereby justify a rotten compromise? And can expediency trump morality and thereby justify a rotten compromise? More specifically, can an appeal to necessity justify the rotten compromise of forced repatriation to Russia? Can an appeal to expediency justify it?

Galsworthy's account is worth mentioning, not just because of its appeal to expediency, but also for its refusal to take an easy way out of the dilemma, namely, by accusing the victims. It was quite common, at the time, especially among pro-Soviet apologists, to accept the Soviet line that those handed over to Russia were all Nazi collaborators, traitors to their country, who deserved what they got at Stalin's hands. The most celebrated case in support of the apologia is that of General Andrey Andreyevich Vlasov, a former Red Army general who fought with great distinction in the first year of the war, fell into the hands of the Germans, turned against the Soviets, and served the Nazi regime by recruiting an army to fight the Soviets, alongside Nazi forces. Then there was the case of Russian prisoners of war compelled by the Germans to wear German uniforms and join the Germans. They served mainly as forced labor or were tempted into it just to escape the harsh conditions imposed on Soviet prisoners of war. Whatever we think about them, not all, not even most, of the people subjected to forced repatriation were of this kind. Referring to all the victims as basically Vlasov's followers is nothing but a convenient distortion.

A Plea of Necessity

Here is the plea: The Allies were engaged in a total war. Their aim was the unconditional surrender of Nazi Germany. Whatever was needed to secure this aim was and is morally justified, given the high moral stakes of defeating Germany. Keeping the alliance going was a necessary condition for achieving total victory over Germany, and anything that endangered the alliance had to be avoided at all costs. To keep the alliance going, the West thought it necessary to go along with the Russians, even if it meant the forced repatriation of prisoners of war. It was a compromise, they argued, in the service of a very good moral cause; it was a fair moral price to pay. If detractors are determined to call this compromise rotten, so be it, but the compromise was justified even if rotten, justified by necessity.

So much for the plea of necessity. Now for the reaction: There is very little question that Nazi Germany was the aggressor in the Second World War. There is no question that the Allies' going to war was justified on the ground of self-defense. But by the end of 1943, at the time of the Tehran conference among the "Big Three"—Stalin, Roosevelt, and Churchill—the dynamics of the war had changed, especially after the decisive Battle of Kursk. At that time, there was no longer much question as to which side would win; the only remaining questions were when and how. This does not mean that the war was over, or that the Big Three felt it was over. There was still a great deal to be concerned about. The German army, still formidable, could no longer reverse the tide of war, and the Allies' plea of self-defense at that stage had already started to wear thin. The very nature of the Yalta conference, a discussion of the future of Europe after the war, attests that by then the Allies did not view Nazi Germany as a serious existential threat. The Allies hadn't caught the tiger yet, but they were already busy dividing its skin. The question is: can a plea of necessity be made in good faith when there is no serious existential threat to the pleaders?

I maintain that the case of Nazi Germany should be treated as a special case. It has to do with the justification for mounting a total war against Germany not based merely on the necessity for self-defense. Indeed, just-war theory is pretty good at telling us when going to war is justified. But the theory is poorly equipped to tell us what to do when there is a change in the dynamics of the war, such as when, by virtue of doing well in the war, the bullied underdog of yesterday is the strong overdog of today.

In a normal war a change in dynamics might change the moral status of the protagonists. A successful underdog may be required to accept an offer to end the war tendered by the losing overdog, even though that same offer coming before the war would have robbed the underdog of its justification for going to war. If it was not a justification to begin with, it cannot be a justification for continuing the war. The underdog is entitled to request compensation for the aggression, but it is not justified in continuing the war for the sake of a mere punitive mission.

This may avail in a normal war, but the war with Nazi Germany was not a normal war. It was a war against radical evil. A radical evil should be eradicated, and only the total defeat of Nazi Germany would accomplish that goal. The aim of the Yalta agreement to achieve the unconditional surrender of Nazi Germany and its de-Nazification was morally right.

An appeal to necessity at the Yalta stage does not have the same force as an appeal to self-defense to suspend incompatible moral demands. That necessity kept the alliance together to secure total victory over a radically evil enemy. But then the question is: what would the Western Allies have risked by refusing forced repatriation and insisting on voluntary repatriation? There is not a shred of evidence that this would have ended the alliance with the Soviet Union. The Soviets, truly worried about a separate deal between the West and Nazi Germany, had so much at stake that it is hard to believe they would have risked antagonizing the Allies on this issue. A refusal of forced repatriation would undoubtedly have put a strain on the relations between the Soviets and the West. It would have created nervousness and suspicion on the part of the Soviets, beyond their already considerable suspicion of the West. True, the Nazi leadership still sought to drive a wedge between the Western Allies and the Soviet Union in the hope of signing a separate peace. Each side had good reason to suspect the other of making a deal with the Nazis, for each side had done so before: Britain in Munich, and the

Soviet Union in the Ribbentrop-Molotov agreement. Yet the right of asylum for prisoners of war would not have ruined the alliance, but only strained it a bit more. To refrain from straining relations at the time was an act of political convenience rather than one of political necessity.

Another worry was more substantial: the Russians might retaliate against the West's refusal to repatriate by force by delaying the return of the British and American prisoners of war captured by the Russians. They were believed at the time to number about fifty thousand (it turned out actually to be half that number). This posed a serious question: how much are you entitled to sacrifice the welfare of your soldiers, in order to safeguard the right of asylum for others, many of whom were your enemies? After the war Eden wrote, "My dominant concern was for the return of our prisoners of war from East Prussia and Poland and I was not prepared to take any action that would jeopardize this."[13] Again, there is not a shred of evidence that the Russians threatened reprisal, though no one doubted they were capable of it. Be that as it may, Eden brought up a very different concern during the war that raises the nagging suspicion that his true reason for agreeing to forced repatriation was, as he brutally expressed it, "If these men do not go back to Russia, where can they go? We don't want them here."[14] So on Eden's mind were neither the necessity for self-defense nor any effort to secure the speedy return of British and American prisoners of war but the desire "not to be saddled with [Soviet prisoners of war] permanently."[15] "We cannot afford being sentimental about it" was Eden's conclusion. Equating the moral and the sentimental—as a form of indulgent attitude in the face of the harsh reality of politics—is a rhetorical gambit used quite frequently in discussions on the relation between politics and morality.

It is clear that all the considerations mentioned played a role, differently with different people. Sir P. J. Grigg, the secretary of state for war, wrote to Eden: "We are in an obvious dilemma. If we do as the Russians want and hand over all these prisoners to them whether or not the prisoners are willing to go back to Russia, we are, as Selborne's minutes of July 25 suggest, sending some of them to their death. And though in war we cannot, as you point out, afford to be sentimental, I confess that I find the prospect rather revolting and I should expect public opinion to reflect the same."[16]

Operation Keelhaul, in the broad sense of the term, covering the whole "operation" of forced repatriation, continued after the war—in fact, till 1947. Even if we accept the necessity argument for the period of the war, there is no justification for accepting it in the peace that followed. True, the agreement was signed during the war, but its implementation, at least in part, took place thereafter. By then the question was whether to keep to the terms of the agreement, rather than whether to sign the agreement.

For the sake of peace, I argued, one should sometimes keep unjust agreements. But whatever the general strength of the argument in favor of keeping an agreement for the sake of peace, it is not clear that it holds in the case of the Yalta agreement, since an Iron Curtain was already drawn across Europe, and keeping to the agreement would not have changed the reality of the Cold War. It may very well be that Eden believed he was concluding the Yalta agreement for the sake of peace with Stalin's Russia. Eden was a ferocious opponent of the Munich agreement and did not believe anything Hitler said. But he believed that he could deal with Stalin, not because Stalin was moral, but because he was prudent. If true, this may explain why Eden was in favor of the agreement during the war, but I am talking about the period after the war, when the Allies had already drifted apart and peace had turned into cold war.

It was right and proper to provide the Soviet Union, which then carried the main burden of the war, with a sense of security. Yet handing over prisoners of war against their will should not have been a part of it. It would have been more just to violate the rotten agreement on forced repatriation than to obey it. In the repatriation agreement, Britain and the United States were both silent partners, but they were also pretty active in aiding and abetting the Soviets by handing over the prisoners. Thus they were more than passive partners to a rotten agreement; they contributed actively to what actually happened to the prisoners. They met something akin to the definition in criminal law of "aiding and abetting," namely, fulfilling the condition of assisting crime perpetrators, so as to be regarded as an essential party to the crime.[17]

The overall impression from the Yalta case is that the West's acquiescence in the demand of the Soviets for forced repatriation was, in the end, not a matter of necessity but a matter of expediency—smoothing things over. Expediency does not trump rottenness. There was no justification or even any excuse for the forced repatriation.

Rotten Compromise and Expressive Politics

What about the other part of the Yalta agreement, which for many cold warriors was the West's betrayal of Eastern Europe? There was a strong tendency to settle scores with those who appeared "soft on communism." As far as rotten compromises are concerned, it is a question of being soft, not on communism, but on Stalinism. Stalinism was a clear case of a regime of cruelty and humiliation.

The years in Stalingrad between 1942 and 1946, much like those between 1917 and the early twenties, were, in E. P. Thompson's words, a period that revealed "the most human face of communism." By his account, for the years that preceded the Yalta agreement—unlike, say, the thirties—there is no justification for viewing Stalinism as a regime of cruelty and humiliation, let alone a clear case of such a regime. Leszek Kolakowksi forcefully questions the aptness of Thompson's "human-face" account with respect to the years 1942–1946: "Do you mean the deportation of eight entire nationalities of the Soviet Union with hundreds of thousands of victims (let us say seven, not eight; one was deported shortly before Stalingrad)? Do you mean sending to concentration camps hundreds of thousands of Soviet prisoners of war handed over by the Allies? Do you mean the so-called 'collectivization' of the Baltic countries, if you have any idea about the reality of this word?"[18] Yet it is true that the war years in the Soviet Union, compared to the years before the war, were morally better. Better, but not good enough to preclude their being described as years of a cruel and humiliating regime.

I do not want to go over everything that was agreed in Yalta. More important, I do not want to go over what was not agreed in Yalta. On the whole, very little that was agreed in Yalta had not been agreed previously: in Casablanca (January 1943), in the Fourth Moscow Conference, with the famous pencil-scribbled division between Churchill and Stalin (October 1944), and in Tehran (November 1944). There was one important difference: at the time of Yalta, the Red Army was already in control of or on the verge of controlling Eastern and Central Europe. The Yalta agreement did not establish the military reality on the ground. It is also clear that it could not change that military reality. The West was at best a sleeping partner to that part of the agreement, not a silent partner. Moreover, in Yalta the Big Two squeezed a promise from Stalin that the liberated people in Europe would be free to choose their government. As it happened, this declaration of liberation was worthless. Stalin never took it seriously, and Churchill knew that Stalin would not take the declaration seriously.

There was nothing rotten in the wording of the Yalta agreement. Wording is important, because rotten compromises matter for *expressive* politics, even when they do not matter for *effective* politics. Effective politics is an undertaking with a high probability of bringing about an intended policy. Expressive politics is doing things that do not affect the outcome in the foreseeable future but merely express an attitude toward the outcome, be it a negative attitude of protest or a positive attitude of support. Insofar as I am an individual citizen, my political engagement is almost always expressive, and so is yours. Even my act of voting in a democratic state, where votes are counted in earnest, is an act of expressive politics: my vote has no chance of making a difference. The outcome of an election is unaffected by my vote. As individuals, we may belong to a group with an effective impact on politics, but each individual alone lacks such causal impact.

One may refuse to call expressive acts "political," in the belief that politics requires constant engagement with power, that is, with policies and acts meant to be causally efficacious. To give up on power is to give up on politics, and to confuse politics with other pursuits, such as aesthetics. Not being involved with real power or not actively pursuing real power is not being serious about politics.

Here is a line of thought I owe to Saul Kripke.[19] You say that you do not believe in expressive politics, which you regard as mere empty gestures. You say that you strongly prefer, say, Obama to McCain, but that your vote for Obama would not make any significant difference. You say that you do not have enough of a reason to go to vote since your vote does not affect the outcome of the election. But you also say that a thousand dollars would have caused you to change your mind, would have been enough of an incentive for you to vote—for Obama, of course. But then, if your vote does not make any significant difference, and the only reason for you to go to vote is the thousand dollars, would you have voted for McCain, had you been guaranteed a thousand dollars for your vote? If you reject the last offer, then no matter what you declare, you are a believer in expressive politics.

How does all of this talk about expressive politics fare in our case concerning the Western Allies? The Western Allies could do very little in Yalta to loosen the grip of Stalin on Eastern Europe. Moreover, the sticky issue of the future government of Poland seemed to be settled when Stalin promised to hold free and unfettered elections, much as Churchill demanded. Yet on his return from Yalta, after a dinner at Chequers, Churchill was, as his trusted secretary John Colville wrote, "rather depressed, thinking of the possibilities of Russia one day turning against us, saying that Chamberlain had trusted Hitler as he was now trusting Stalin."[20] So a possible damaging comparison between Yalta and Munich did not escape Churchill. Munich was a part of effective politics. Hitler might have been stopped then and there. But the destiny of Eastern Europe would have been very much the same, with or without the Yalta agreement. The Western Allies were mere sleeping partners to the agreement. Yalta, unlike Munich, was an exercise in expressive politics. It was not really an exercise in effective politics.

The question is: should we be morally disturbed when a sleeping partner signs a rotten compromise for its own advantage? If the rotten compromise asked of the sleeping partner is nothing but an exercise in expressive politics, as the relevant part of the Yalta agreement probably was, why is it so absolutely wrong?

The distinction between expressive and effective politics holds in the short run and in the middle run, but is markedly less compelling in the long run. On too many occasions, the protest of today is the commonsense policy of tomorrow: what is expressive today may turn out to be effective in the long run. Thus expressive politics can be viewed as a bet on the future, the remote future.

Yalta involved recognizing borders. Recognizing borders is never a mere piece of expressive politics. William Ralph Inge, the shrewd dean of St. Paul, famously said, "A man may build himself a throne of bayonets, but he cannot sit on it."[21] Even the most brutal of regimes tries to achieve recognition for its hold on a certain territory. Legitimacy is an overused word, but it is what people in power ask for, at times, from people without power. The reasons are complicated, but the fact of trying to gain legitimacy is not. Thus expressive politics has some *soft* power to constrain *hard* power. Inge is, to my mind, off the beam in saying, "It is useless for sheep to pass resolutions in favor of vegetarianism, while the wolf remains of different opinion."[22] The wolf is not indifferent. It knows that sheep's resolutions might matter in the long run.

People's consciousness holds a moral record of some world events. This fact is part of power politics, not just a moral fact. Having signed a rotten compromise is an egregious item in a nation's moral record. This is perhaps why Munich keeps haunting us. The reason is that a rotten compromise is made at the expense of the two main constitutive elements of morality: avoidance of humiliation and of cruelty. Because it touches these two elements, the moral requirement to avoid rotten compromises is so demanding that it holds even when it concerns, in the short run, nothing but expressive politics.

"Come What May"

Whether to reach a compromise is left for us to decide. But what is not left to us, morally, is to decide whether to reach a rotten compromise. We face a stringent injunction: Thou shall not commit a rotten compromise, come what may.

But what is the force of the "come what may" clause?

It seems that the "come what may" clause is very strong, not just rhetorically, but also normatively. Normative Judaism recognizes injunctions specially designed for times of persecution. In such times, one is reduced to obeying the minimum required for moral (religious) life. According to Jewish law one should not give in to three imperatives, come what may: murder, incest, and idolatry. The "come what may" clause means that one should be ready to be killed rather than transgress the three requirements just mentioned. These are the Jewish imperatives for behavior under duress.

But what if an individual transgresses and kills an innocent to save his own life? Is he a murderer who should be punished by death? The right attitude toward a person who under duress kills an innocent to save his own life is subject to controversy. In Maimonides' view, the issue is clear: one should not be punished by law. "It need not be said that he is not executed by a court of law even if he was forced to commit murder."[23]

The idea is that although one is never justified in killing the innocent, even under duress, the circumstances are such that we can *understand* him. There is a normative expectation that one would obey the injunction and be killed rather than transgress. But there is an empirical observation that one may fail by finding the pressure too much to bear. The attitude is this: We understand. We do not *justify* and we do not even *excuse*, but we *understand*. We understand one's failure, knowing that we might fail in similar circumstances. Hence it is not for us to punish the transgressor. At most, we are entitled to feel disappointed that the person did not resist, but we are not entitled to punish.

This complicated attitude of hoping for the best and expecting the worst could serve us well in how to react toward one who has made a rotten compromise. Understanding is less than excusing and forgiving. It is, however, based on an intense recognition of human frailty and vulnerability. For that, I turned to religious moral experience. It has an advantage over secular morality in that it recognizes human frailty as an essential element of morality. Indeed, the attitude I advocate with regard to rotten compromise is that making a rotten compromise as a passive partner cannot be justified—in the sense that I am committed to the "come what may" clause—but it may nonetheless be understood and even excused.

The "come what may" clause is caught between two conflicting positions. On the one hand, we recognize that cruelty and humiliation are fundamentally evil. Their avoidance is constitutive of the moral order itself, and so the injunction not to agree to a regime of cruelty and humiliation should have the widest possible scope: hence the "come what may" clause. On the other hand, the "come what may" clause has a rather daunting effect when attached to the injunction "Do not compromise in favor of cruelty and humiliation." It seems at odds with the spirit of compromise, which by its very nature is the negation of the unyielding spirit of "come what may."

In ideal theory, where agents are motivated to pursue justice, there is no fear of a rotten compromise. The injunction to refrain from contracting a rotten compromise is almost by definition advanced with reference to a nonideal situation. Yet the absolute nature of the demand to avoid rotten compromises at all costs seems like an injunction coming from ideal theory.

Second Best and Compromise

The spirit of my moral dealings with compromise is captured by the phrase Reinhold Niebuhr coined in the title of his *Moral Man and Immoral Society*, namely, what a moral agent, motivated to act morally, must do in two different settings: first, in an *indifferent* moral society; second, in an *immoral* society.[24] Society, here, may include the society of nations, not just a society that comprises individuals. This is why I use the highfalutin term "agent" to cover both individuals and groups.

To my understanding, the injunction "Do not make a rotten compromise, come what may," should be situated in a nonideal moral context, even if the absolutist tone of "come what may" seems to belong to the repertoire of ideal theory. I do not object to ideal theory as such, on the ground that it is ideal. Ideal gas theory has its use, even though nothing in nature has perfect elasticity and no volume. In normal conditions—when the pressure is not too high and the temperature is not too low—the behavior of ideal gas approximates rather well the behavior of real gas.

But humans do not behave like atoms of gas. And the dialectic between the ideal and the real works differently in the case of humans. This is well represented by what economists call second-best theories. Let me return to and elaborate this theme of the second best, which I have addressed in my introduction.

If, for example, we are prevented from attaining one or more of the conditions necessary to reach the "ideal," we should not behave as if the ideal conditions hold, in hopes of attaining at least the second-best goal. It may very well be the case that in order to attain that second-best goal, we should adopt a different course of action from the one prescribed by the ideal theory. If, for example, during trading, one of the Pareto conditions for a perfect market does not hold, we should not assume that we have to trade as if the market were perfect, so as to attain, at least, the second-best result. To attain the second best, we might be required to do something very different.

The Catholic Church believes that being a nun is the ideal life. It is the life of perfection for women. The Catholic Church also believes that the sacrifice entailed in giving up sexuality and motherhood is such that most women cannot attain the ideal of becoming nuns. The second best for a woman is not to become a nun with a lax attitude toward the prohibition of sexuality, but instead to become a mother.

There is a sense that our basic compromise between the real material life we lead and the ideal life is a compromise that inherently opts for second best. It is the ultimate second best, second to the ideal best. Bertrand Russell is not far off the mark when he writes, "Real life is, to most men, a long second best, a perpetual compromise between the ideal and the possible but the world of pure reason knows no compromise, no practical limitations, no barrier to the creative activity."[25] Russell's idea is that the real material world is based on scarcity, hence the need to compromise. The spiritual world of pure reason is abundant: in the absence of limitation, there is no need to compromise.

Indeed, thinkers like Maimonides preferred the Aristotelian ideal of the contemplative life to the active, material life. His reason was that the life of the mind suffers no scarcity.

The stuff of the life of the mind, the spirit, is unlimited; the stuff of material life, matter, is limited. Real life, that is, life constrained by material existence, forces us to lead a compromised life. The idea in any case is that leading a non-contemplative life, the kind of life most of the human race leads, is already a tremendous compromise. But what is more troubling is that even our moral life, our good moral life, looks like a tattered compromise.

The idea beyond this notion is simple. The suffering in this world is so intense that it should burden us with a moral obligation to alleviate it. And the claim on us is so strong that nothing but a total dedication to assuaging the anguish in the world exempts us from fulfilling the required moral life. Moral life should be nothing short of saintly life. Given the suffering in the world, how can we justify any of our indulgent pursuits, if by the same effort we could help people in desperate need? By not leading the life that many people associate, rightly or wrongly, with the life of Mother Teresa, we already compromise ourselves. To dilute morality in the name of the realism of the second best is to compromise doubly.

The last remarks on the relation between compromise and the second best do not amount to establishing a *conceptual* connection between compromise and the idea of the second best, but they are enough to suggest an *intimate* relation between the two, the point being that the spirit of compromise is the spirit of resigning oneself to the idea of the second best.

Where "Come What May" Comes From

I locate the source of the clause "come what may" in ideal theory, and the source of our troubles with this clause in our attempts to apply ideal theory to nonideal situations. But another source suggests itself most strongly, a very different source: from theory based on the idea that certain sorts of deeds are wrong in themselves and should be avoided, no matter what their consequences are. Such a theory originates not to achieve best or second-best goals, but to avoid doing what is wrong in and of itself. A moral theory directed to achieving the good goal (*telos*) was called "teleological," whereas a theory guided not by goals but by the duty (*deon*) to do the right thing irrespective of the consequences was called "deontological." The "come what may" clause suits a deontological theory dealing with what is right, rather than with what is good, best, or second-best.

A standard complaint against deontological theories is that it is not clear under what principles some actions are wrong in and of themselves. Thus we face a list like the Ten Commandments, and we are told this we should not do, no matter what, but without a sense of why those items are on the list. A possible answer is that we do not need general principles to make the list clearer, since the items on the list are much clearer than any general principle: we understand that we should not kill, torture, or rape better than we understand any general principle.

But whatever the list of things to be avoided comes to, we do not expect to find among them the injunction "Thou shall not contract a rotten compromise." Such a list may tell us that we should avoid humiliation and cruelty, but this is an injunction directed at the active partner to a rotten agreement—the one who actually inflicts cruelty and humiliation—and hardly an injunction directed to the passive partner, the one who agrees to a regime of cruelty and humiliation without inflicting it.

The deontological list of don'ts is a micromorality list. It does not include don'ts for governments. The relevant list for our concern is a macromorality list. This list is highly problematical, since there is a tendency to exempt governments from the don'ts, the implication being that provided they act in the public interest and not in their own private interest, government officials are allowed to dirty their hands.

Instead of Conclusion

I am not yet ready to conclude. The relation between political necessity and rotten compromise will also be at the core of my next chapter.

-5-

THE MORALITY OF ROTTEN COMPROMISES

Dirty Hands between Ethics and Morality

"MY BROTHER AND I are against my cousin. My cousin and I are against the whole world" is a Bedouin proverb. It captures the human condition much better than does Plautus's proverb, made famous by Hobbes, that "man is wolf to man."

The succinct Bedouin proverb expresses a powerful picture of human life and politics, a picture that for obvious reasons I shall call *tribalism*. Tribalism is the idea that solidarity is based solely on the closeness of blood relations. It is intensified by a state of permanent hostility to the rest of the world. Tribalism suggests a much-needed distinction between two types of human relations: *thick relations* versus *thin relations*. Thick relations are relations like those with family members. Thin relations are relations with strangers.

Tribalism is one form of thick relations, a blood relation, an extension of family relations. Tribalism conveys the traditional notion of thick relations. The modern notion of close relations stresses voluntary relations such as friendship. In thick relations there is depth, created by shared memories. In thin relations there is very little memory.

Based on the distinction between thick and thin human relations, I draw a distinction between *ethics* and *morality*.[1] Ethics regulates our thick relations, while morality regulates our thin relations. A society can in principle be ethical and immoral: such a society finds close relations a binding force, and the sense of shared humanity a very weak force. This is a typical case of tribalism. Indeed, ethics without moral constraints is tribalism.

Aryan Nazi Germany was an ethical society with regard to its fellow Germans, and a deeply immoral society with regard to humanity at large.[2] Here is a baffling question: did Hitler have ethical relations with his fellow Germans? My short answer is no.

My long answer calls for some explanation. To the extent that the distinction between close and distant relations has political force, it goes beyond face-to-face relations: it is extended to people whom we have never met. In short, we extrapolate our thick relations way beyond face-to-face relations. This is the mental exercise for which Benedict Anderson coined the label "imagined community."[3] An imagined community is imagined in terms of the persons we include as fellow members and also in terms of the characteristics that we ascribe to them.

In the case of Hitler, it is very clear that his beliefs about the German people had very little to do with who they were. At the end of the war, the actual Germans disappointed him by not living up to his fervent expectations; hence he thought they deserved annihilation. Anyone whose relations with his fellow members do not mesh seriously with reality has no thick relations with them.

An imagined society is not a fanciful society. It resembles those with whom we have face-to-face relations. What we ascribe to the imagined members, even if idealized, cannot be entirely divorced from real-world characteristics. By this account, the delusional Don Quixote has no thick relations with the peasant girl Aldonza Lorenzo, whom, in his fervent imagination, he turned into his lady-love Dulcinea. Nor would I describe Don Quixote as having thin relations with the windmills that he believed were ferocious giants. An imagined community cannot, for the sake of ethics, be a delusional community.

As for Hitler, his attitude to the Germans was neither ethical nor moral, but delusional. This is not true, on the whole, for most members of Nazi Germany. They had ethical relations with their imagined fellow Germans, and immoral relations with the rest of humanity.[4] The dual nature of human relations as codified by ethics and morality invites tension: ethics at the expense of morality, but also morality at the expense of ethics.

A group guided by strong ethics can be extremely selfish in facing other collectives and individuals, yet individuals in the group may show a great readiness to sacrifice for the sake of their community. Such ethical individuals, however, expect their community to act most selfishly in defending the interests of the collective. For them, defending the interests of the community is the ultimate imperative. The unselfishness of ethical individuals, in an ethical and immoral society, gives them the illusion that they belong to a moral order, since they identify morality with individual unselfishness. But then they may feel no moral compunctions if their leaders sign a rotten compromise at the expense of a third party, provided such a compromise furthers the interests of their group.

The ethical and immoral picture of politics is an admixture of strong tribalism and an international Hobbesian jungle. Tribalism is widespread. It is not confined to some unruly parts of Afghanistan and Pakistan, but ranges to societies that look very different from bearded tribal societies, and whose members might be clean-shaven.[5]

According to the tribal picture of ethics without morality, a rotten compromise has a very different meaning from the moral picture: a compromise is rotten only if it arises from betrayal perpetrated by leaders selling out the vital interests of the group for personal gain. But a compromise concluded by community leaders for the sake of the collective, and not for personal gain, is viewed by the tribalist as utterly justified. Leaders' hands can do the dirty work on our behalf and get dirty, much as garbage collectors' hands get dirty on our behalf. Unselfishness is the soap that cleans dirty hands.

The opposite attitude to ethical tribalism is the moral attitude expressed by the slogan "not in our name." We refuse to accept dirty deeds (immoral deeds) done by dirty hands for our sake. "Not in our name" is a way of dissociating ourselves from dirty hands. Biblically put (after Genesis 22:27), it is a refusal to accept an immoral division of labor between the voice of Jacob ("our moral name") and the hands of Esau (the dirty, immoral hands allegedly acting on our behalf).

Not in Our Name

Deontological theories have considerable force in micro-morality but lose their *psychological* grip in the context of macromorality. More precisely, this occurs under the following conditions. We encounter the public sentiment telling the government "not in our name" when a government, supposed to represent us, does immoral things that it should not do. If it does them nevertheless, we dissociate ourselves from the government's deed, declaring that the wrong was not done in our name. The "we" is meant in the sense of "we the people." But what it really means is "we the moral opposition to the government."

It does not always mean that. On occasion the scope of "not in our name" is broader than "the moral opposition," and the "we" truly becomes "we the people." It happens when "we the people" are not in danger. In such circumstances we can afford to be moral, aspire to do right and refrain from doing wrong, even at some cost to ourselves. But when facing a significant adverse prospect that we perceive as a threat to our way of life, let alone to our very lives, "we the people" have very little patience with claims about right and wrong, irrespective of their outcomes. In such cases ethical tribalism runs deeper than morality.

Let me rephrase the last observation. The relation we bear to a legitimate government is that of *principal* to *agent*. We, the people, are the principal; the government is the agent, employed to act on behalf of the principal. The relation is such that the agent can contract on behalf of the principal, in ways that bind the principal. The expectation is that the agent should act in the principal's best interests. When there is a clash between moral principles and the principal's interests (narrowly conceived), the public ("we the people") is ready to hear moral claims, even in cases where doing wrong is advantageous. But the public turns a deaf ear when what is morally wrong is perceived as the only effective way to stop a significant adverse outcome. The public is ready to set moral constraints in cases involving gains, but rather reluctant to do so in cases involving significant losses.

Not that in trying to avoid losses, the public loses its morality. I do not claim that. What I do claim is that in adverse situations, the public expects morality to be sensitive to the outcome of its policy. Utter disregard for outcomes in such cases is taken as a sign of unbearable *moralism*, that is to say, an exaggerated emphasis on morality at the expense of politics. Public sentiment can be crudely summarized: in gaining, allow yourself to be Kantian; in losing, be selfishly utilitarian—taking only your utilities into account.

My claim, in other words, is not that deontological morality ("Kantian" morality) is irrelevant in the public domain, and only relevant in the private domain. My claim is that there is a psychological asymmetry between the public perception of morality in the face of a favorable outcome, and its perception in the face of an adverse outcome. In the face of an adverse outcome, the public insists on assessing the consequences, and is relatively unwilling to be constrained by the niceties of doing what is right in and of itself.

The clause "come what may" covers adverse outcomes. However, this is exactly the situation in which the public is reluctant to listen to injunctions of the form "Do not do X, for the sole reason that it is morally wrong to do X, come what may." The pressure is to devise a formula in which the consequences of what we do are taken into account. But such a formula does not fit well with the clause "come what may."

Political morality is morality applied to political circumstances. If my observation is valid as to the asymmetry between the relative willingness to behave morally in situations of gain and the relative unwillingness to do so in situations of loss, should our behavior be such as never to ignore the consequences of our policy?

I suggest a distinction between the theory of the right and the theory of the good with respect to rotten compromises. The theory of the right tells us that there is no justification for a rotten compromise under any circumstances, irrespective of its consequences for those who sign it. The theory of the good tells us that although there is no justification for a rotten compromise, there is room for forgiveness or at least understanding, depending on the consequences of such a compromise.

Compromise between the Prescriptive and the Normative

Let us distinguish between two types of moral policy: *normative* policy and *prescriptive* policy. By "policy" I understand guiding principles, which inform decision and action. Normative policy is designed to be carried out in a moral society, a society populated by agents motivated to bring about and maintain, as their overriding concern, a just society.

Prescriptive moral policy is designed for a nonmoral society. In a normative theory your path in life is lighted by a powerful blazing projector; in a prescriptive theory your immediate path is lighted by a miner's dim headlamp.

There are two kinds of nonmoral societies: an *indifferent society* and an *immoral society*. In an indifferent moral society, people act for diverse kinds of reasons, among them moral reasons. People in an indifferent society do not regard moral reasons as particularly weighty, let alone give morality the exalted status of supplying an overriding consideration. An indifferent society can be highly legalistic: it may take legal considerations seriously yet be indifferent to moral considerations.

In calling a society morally indifferent, I do not mean that it is utterly indifferent to morality. That society is only relatively indifferent between moral considerations and other kinds of considerations; all considerations are on equal footing. That society does not give morality its proper due. In short, a morally indifferent society is one we are most likely to encounter most of the time, in most places, and inhabited by the greatest number of people.

In contrast, an immoral society is an extreme case because it utterly disregards moral considerations. Nazi Germany made the difference between an indifferent and an immoral society a difference in kind rather than in degree. Nazi Germany, like the proverbial Sodom and Gomorrah, is a society that actively sets out to undermine morality itself.

Compromise is the stuff of *prescriptive* theory. Yet rotten compromise is a category of *normative* theory. It puts a normative constraint on acceptable compromises. A rotten compromise is, categorically, an unacceptable compromise.

Urgency and Emergency

When the formula "come what may" is attached to a moral policy that consists of rules, what contingencies should it cover? The question seems odd since the whole point of this emphatic formula is to cover anything and everything that we can imagine. But rules of any kind are massively dependent on a tacit assumption of normalcy, an assumption of business as usual. The priest who looks up the rules of baptism tacitly and unwittingly assumes that he is not going to face—in the spirit of Locke's discussion[6]—a newborn with two heads, and need to decide whether he should dip the baby once or twice or not at all. Rules cannot cover all possible cases: they are inherently subject to open interpretation, that is to say, when applied to possibly difficult and vague cases. We may safely assume that the rules governing baptism are not made with such freak cases in mind. What counts as abnormal with respect to rules varies greatly from context to context, and from practice to practice.

In the case of moral rules we face a dilemma. On the one hand, we need moral rules to guide us in extremely abnormal cases, as in the case of war. On the other hand, just such an abnormal situation as war makes normal moral rules lose their grip.

For Carl Schmitt there is no dilemma.[7] Morality in abnormal situations does not make sense. For Schmitt, moral or legal rules do not hold in the face of exceptions. Morality and legalism are replaced by the political ability to make brute decisions. Brute in two senses: unguided by rules and principles, but also in the sense of brutal. For Schmitt, a state of war is a paradigmatic case of emergency, in which political considerations should silence any other principled behavior.[8]

Leaving aside Schmitt, the question for us is whether an abnormal situation is an emergency that calls for a suspension of morality. More specifically, since rotten compromises, unlike normal compromises, are usually made in abnormal times, shouldn't this fact limit the scope of "come what may" to normal times?

Morality and Abnormality

There are two germane senses of "abnormality" with regard to moral policy: abnormality in the sense of freaks of nature, and abnormality in the sense of the unexpected. Wars are abnormal in the second sense, if we devise our policy for peacetimes without, for the sake of our policy, taking wars into account.

Wars are far from being freakish. They are a familiar part of life. But they differ radically from situations of peace, for which our normal policies are devised. I mention war as a case of abnormality since rotten compromises have a great deal to do with war. We may look at war the way we look at a butterfly. It goes through three completely different phases: caterpillar, pupa, and adult butterfly (imago). Each and every adult butterfly goes through these stages; there is no abnormality here. But these three stages look so utterly different that one wonders whether what we say about the adult butterfly holds for the pupa? Indeed, a similar question keeps haunting us with regard to human fetuses. Do they represent a radically different phase, or are they on a continuum with adult human beings? "Come what may," too, may be relative to a phase—say, the phase of peace—and inapplicable to the phase of war. Or "Come what may" may be relative to the kind of society we are dealing with. Is it a moral society, an indifferent society, or an immoral society?

Abnormality, as a problem for applying a rule, has mainly to do with abnormality in the freakish sense of the word, namely, being conspicuously dissimilar, being like nothing else. "Come what may" is not meant to cover any imaginable possibility, but only realistic possibilities. There are two senses of realistic scenarios: one is akin to realism in art, that is, lifelike description, unlikely but not bizarre; another is realistic in the sense of having a significant probability of occurrence, likely but not lifelike. A description can be very vivid and lifelike, rich in details the way life is, but the more lifelike details we add, the less likely it is. We are very likely to meet a man with two eyes, a nose, and a mouth, but such a schematic description is neither vivid nor lifelike. If, however, we add that he has a scar on his left cheek, we make the description more vivid and more lifelike, but we are much less likely to meet such a person.

What correlates realism in the two senses—lifelike and likely—is dealing with real historical cases, rather than thought experiments. So hedging our "come what may" to realistic possibilities does not free us from facing hard cases that actually happen, such as wars. It does free us from covering freakish situations. A pact with the devil, in the literal sense, is a freakish case. The "come what may" appended to "do not sign a rotten compromise" does not cover pacts with the devil in the mythic sense of the expression. But then pacts with the devil in the metaphorical sense do exist, and they are not necessarily freak cases.

Here is an important use of the metaphor "pact with the devil." Yisrael Kastner was head of the Jewish organization known as the Aid and Rescue Committee during the Nazi occupation of Hungary. He made a deal with Adolf Eichmann, the SS officer in charge of the deportation of Hungarian Jews to death camps. The agreement saved 1,685 souls, who fled Hungary by what was later known as Kastner's train. In Eichmann's account of the deal in *Life* magazine, Kastner "agreed to help keep the Jews from resisting deportation." "It was a good bargain," Eichmann said, meaning that it was good for the Germans.[9]

After the war, Kastner moved to Israel, where he was accused in a published pamphlet of collaboration with the Nazis. The accuser was sued for libel. Judge Benjamin Halevi wrote: "The Nazis' patronage of Kastner, and their agreement to let him save six hundred prominent Jews, were part of the plan to exterminate the Jews. Kastner was given a chance to add a few more to that number. The bait attracted him. The opportunity of rescuing prominent people appealed to him greatly. He considered the rescue of the most important Jews as a great personal success and a success for Zionism. It was a success that would also justify his conduct—his political negotiation with Nazis and the Nazi patronage of his committee. When Kastner received this present from the Nazis, *Kastner sold his soul to the German Satan*" (emphasis added).[10]

Halevi's use of the expression "the German Satan" is purely metaphorical. It does not designate a freak case. By his account, Kastner's pact with the Nazi devil is clearly meant to render it rotten, and it should be covered by the injunction not to sign a rotten compromise.

There is a serious issue regarding whether the agreement between "the German Satan" and Kastner can be regarded as a compromise, given the coercive nature of the deal. The Israeli Supreme Court rejected Halevi's verdict. It refused to view the agreement as rotten, partly because it was coercive. I think the Supreme Court was right and Justice Halevi was wrong, but that is another matter: the point is that freak cases are not covered by morality, whereas mere hard cases in hard circumstances should be covered.

My general point is that wars and emergencies are extreme situations from the point of view of peace. But they are not abnormal in the freak sense of the term, even if metaphorically we tend to describe them as such. Rules, moral rules included, can apply to wars as well as to compromises made in times of war. The whole idea of a just-war theory, which advocates justice in the conduct of war, is that the open violence of war can be regulated and subjected to constraints. War is a different phase in human existence from peace, but not a mode of existence that renders morality irrelevant.

Indeed, the idea that behavior in war can and should be regulated (by norms, though not necessarily moral norms) has ancient sources. For one thing, in the conduct of war, an old concern was to preserve a code of honor, aristocratic honor, even in violent situations. The old sense of honor is vertical, honor between unequals. The modern concern is with honor in its horizontal form, respect for human beings as humans.

Even in war we are required to treat humans with basic dignity. Humiliation is the denial of that, and cruel humiliation is the severe case of denying humans the moral status of human beings. Basically, what we are asked, in a moral sense, is to take the human dignity of the enemy with the same seriousness once directed to the aristocratic honor of one's noble adversaries.

Easier said than done, in practice, but it is important that it is easier to say, in principle, for it suggests that the idea of treating our enemy without humiliation makes sense. If so, it makes sense to require us in a situation of war not to conclude rotten compromises and not to behave according to the logic of Schmittian exceptions, meant to nullify morality in times of crisis. This would turn the demand to avoid rotten compromises, come what may, into an absurd demand.

One of the ideas associated with our sense of the *absurd* is the idea of behaving as if it were business as usual, when in fact business is very unusual. We recognize it, for example, in Harold Pinter's plays—his use of cozy, soothing clichés in menacing settings. Talking morality in a state of war strikes many as absurd in this Pinteresque sense. It is like behaving in a business-as-usual manner in a situation that is anything but usual.

I maintain that it was never true that applying rules—rules of honor in this case—to war was perceived as absurd. Conduct in war was constrained by considerations of honor even in pressing emergencies and urgencies. Wars as such do not provide a sweeping justification of necessity for contracting rotten compromises.

Civil Wars and Rotten Compromises

There is something misleading in my insistence on bringing up examples from the Second World War. Wars' landscapes have changed dramatically since the Second World War. There is a marked decline in wars among states and a stunning increase of civil wars.

We are in a sense back to the reality of the religious civil war, the reality that shaped Hobbes's philosophy. Hobbes forged a famous picture of an immoral world. I use the expression "immoral world" rather than "immoral society" because the situation Hobbes described as "war of all against all" does not enable us to maintain any form of society. He immortalized life in such an immoral world: "And the life of man, solitary, poor, nasty, brutish and short."[11] This is a puzzling characterization. If life is so terrible, why complain that it is short? Its brevity seems like a redeeming feature.

But this is the least of my concerns with Hobbes's account. The big concern is that war of all against all is not a serious possibility: it is a freak situation. In a total war, in which every individual is a mortal enemy, no one would be able to raise children. Total war of all against all is total annihilation within one short generation. As long as Hobbes's parable is meant to describe individuals warring all the time, it is not fanciful fiction but impossibility.

Hobbes's parable makes sense when the reference is not to individuals but to collectives. Individuals, even in the most wretched situations, need a support system—family, clan, tribe, nation, or friends. We should not take literally a war of all against all. A state of anarchy in a civil war is bad enough. The civil war in Iraq today can serve as a useful reminder of Hobbes's point, whether or not each and every Iraqi or American in Iraq is against each and every other Iraqi or American. What is important in Hobbes's account is the priority of security. Grab security; morality will come later. Security in Hobbes's account is a threshold demand: security overrides all moral considerations.

We should distinguish two doctrines here between which there is serious tension: *moralism* and *reason of state* (better known as *raison d'état*). Moralism is the belief in the primacy of morality over politics—indeed, the primacy of the moral consideration over any other consideration. Reason of state is the doctrine of the primacy of the political over the moral. Hobbes is a doctrinaire of the reason of state.

Raison d'état acquired a bad reputation. Too many cynics and power-mongers acted in its name. It wears a Richelieu-Mephistophelian goatee. Cardinal Richelieu was able both to write an influential guidebook for Christians, and to conclude a series of alliances with Protestants (Swedish, Germans, and Swiss) against his fellow Catholics of the Austro-Spanish Hapsburg dynasty. He was even able to support the Protestants of Canton Grisons in their war against the pope, and all for reasons of state, the state being France, the centralized France he helped shape.[12] Neither Metternich nor Kissinger could better him. But the doctrine was not conceived in sin. It was a response to a serious crisis, the crisis of the religious civil wars in Europe in the sixteenth and seventeenth centuries. Civil wars with a religious bent are so wretched that peace at all costs seems preferable—including serious costs in terms of religious morality.

The idea behind the reason-of-state doctrine was that only an absolutist regime could establish a peace that would free its subjects from the horrors of civil war. Reason of state is first and foremost a set of reasons that override religious morality (morality anchored in religion). Acting on religious morality, according to the doctrine of reason of state, is what fuels civil wars. Religious morality is part of the problem of civil wars; it cannot be its solution. Peace, which is freedom from civil war, should be pursued even at the expense of justice, or any other ideal. The solution is to be found in reason of state, the only reason that can secure peace. Reason of state is instrumental in bringing about freedom from internal civil war, and that is its main justification.[13]

As for wars between states, the doctrine, at the time, faced the reality of a Europe divided among sovereign states, wishing to extend their rule to the rest of the world. The mechanism of securing peace among states is based on the idea of balance of power. Reason of state, as a reason in the service of peace, was conceived to monitor the balance of power so that no state would deviate from the status quo. The status quo should be maintained by diplomacy, if possible, and by force, if necessary.

Absolute power absolutely corrupted the moral fiber of the doctrine of reason of state. It stopped being a doctrine about maintaining peace and became synonymous with state egotism. The moral dimension of the doctrine of reason of state, as a reason to establish and maintain peace, was forgotten for a while. But civil wars and religious civil wars are still with us. Even those whose home is remote from Baghdad can see, if not feel, the horrors of a civil war, coming in the wake of a foreign occupation.

Hobbes, the philosopher of security, forcefully states his challenge: Civil war is what we dread most. Any regime that can secure peace and avoid civil war, even by means of cruelty and humiliation, is a legitimate regime. Such a regime should not be made a moral pariah, since it obeys the basic political requirement of providing freedom from civil war. One should be allowed to deal with such a regime and reach compromises as one deems fit. Any regime that passes the threshold demand of effective security for its subjects and is willing to live in peace with its neighbors is a proper partner to an agreement, even if such an agreement is a rotten compromise.

Hobbes's challenge is relevant—above all, to the question of whether a silent partner can sign an agreement with a rotten government—but is by no means an argument that justifies rotten compromises. Not every compromise with a rotten regime is a rotten compromise. Hobbes provides us with an argument for dealing with rotten regimes, but not an argument for making rotten deals, that is, deals that establish or maintain an order of cruelty and humiliation.

Security as Justification or Excuse

In dealing with the Yalta agreement, I have already raised the issue of security as a justification for a rotten compromise. But I dismissed it on the ground that when the Yalta agreement was signed, the outcome of the war was not in question. By then, there was no existential threat to the Allies. The perception of an existential threat was still very real in January 1943, at Casablanca, when it was agreed that the aim of the war was unconditional German surrender. The argument that Yalta was not a clear case in which an appeal to security could prima facie justify a rotten compromise still leaves us with the question: can security ever serve as a justification for a passive partner to contract a rotten compromise?

Security is a lazy placeholder. It appears to have all the force of an appeal to self-defense, in the justification of the use of immoral means. An appeal to security is all too often misused as a justification for what is morally unjustified and perhaps unjustifiable. The crucial question is what security we should guarantee in order to provide a justification to deviate from moral imperatives in general, and to contract a rotten compromise in particular.

The context we are dealing with is *macromorality*. It consists of relations between collectives. But *micromorality*—relations between individuals—provides the model for our macromoral context. The question is whether the micromoral model is suitable for macromorality.

Plato claimed that the state is an individual writ large. That is, the collective, the state, is a good model for the individual psyche. But our political life is shaped by an opposite tendency, namely, to view relations between collectives, states, on the model of relations between individuals. I am not sure that the similarity of relations between individuals to relations between collectives is more important than their dissimilarity. I do believe, however, that we are in the grip of a very strong picture (an unconscious model) in which relations between individuals model relations between collectives. For example, we refer to states by the names of their leaders. And we describe relations between states as personal relations between their leaders. I find myself using the synecdoche Stalin and Hitler, quite extensively, to refer to the Soviet Union and Nazi Germany, in spite of my objection to the idea of viewing states as individuals.

The appeal to necessity, in individual relations, as a justification for deviating from moral behavior can be divided into three: the necessity of using immoral means to safeguard life; the necessity of safeguarding the material means of life, or what is called the defense of property; and finally the necessity of safeguarding one's home (in fanciful but telling language, one's "castle"). Each one of the three defenses has an important role as a model for understanding collective "necessities." Let me comment briefly on each one. Justification here means applying the term "just" to an act that in normal circumstances is unjust.

Self-defense is justified in saving one's life. Yet necessity covers the saving of a third party, provided that the third party does not consist of family or friends engaged in illegal activities. Alter ego defense—defense of a third party—comes under the justification of necessity. But it does not cover the use—without consent—of a third person to shield oneself from danger. The practice of using human shields, namely, combatants hiding behind unwilling civilians to deter the enemy from attacking them, is morally unacceptable. The practice of using human shields is in no way covered by the justification of self-defense. One can, facing grave danger, ignore the property rights of a third party, but one is not allowed to ignore the right to life of an innocent third party. I stress this case of the third party, in an appeal to necessity, for the obvious reason that it plays an important role in the effort to justify rotten compromises. Is a passive party, in a rotten compromise, who attempts to deflect a danger by contracting a rotten compromise, comparable to the one using a human shield—a morally unjustified act—or are those acceptable violations of third-party property rights, for the sake of avoiding immediate danger?

The idea was that property was not a luxury but one's livelihood, a means to enable human subsistence. An attack on property was perceived as an attack on water supply rather than an attack on luxury goods. I have already mentioned, in my introduction, that impoverishment did not mean what it means today in the developed world: loss of social status and loss of standard of living. It meant something dramatically different: the danger of becoming a slave. Defending property was perceived as defending not the accessories of life but its necessities. The defense of property is not the invention of rapacious capitalism. On the contrary, capitalism severed the immediate relation between property and means of living. To the defense of life and defense of necessary means of life in justifying the use of violence, we should add a third element in micromorality, the defense of one's home, "one's castle."

Acts in defense of life, livelihood, and home serve as micro-models for justifying the use of violence in macromorality, but do these serve us well? More specifically, do they serve us well in the case of rotten compromises? The justifications I mentioned for deviating from standard morality have to do with danger to life or danger to vital means of life. How does all this translate into our concern with rotten compromises? If passive partner A yields to B's pressure to sign a rotten agreement, when A's security would otherwise be threatened by B (security in any of the senses above), then whatever A does cannot be regarded as a compromise. A is under duress, which in any case nullifies the validity of the agreement.

If, however, A uses the agreement to obtain its security from B, by agreeing to a rotten compromise with B at the expense of a third party C, then A uses C as a shield. In such a case the justification of self-defense does not hold. Using a bystander as a shield is never justified, not even when the threat to life is serious. A rotten compromise used as a shield is no justification, not even if it is made under a serious threat. A serious threat may, however, provide an excuse, and even a compelling excuse—an excuse that leaves us little choice but to grant forgiveness.

The Tragic Choice between Moral and Ethical Conflict

Morality is the undertaking to regulate human relations between human beings. Human beings should also establish humane relations with animals, but that is a different undertaking. Rotten compromise undermines the very undertaking of morality. It helps bring about a regime of inhuman relations. Cruel humiliation is the act of undermining human relations. Ethics is the undertaking of regulating thick human relations. The two basic models for thick relations are family and friends.

A great deal of thought, and I hasten to add, anxiety, surrounds the question of whether there are genuine moral dilemmas, where an agent is morally required to do A, and also morally required to do B, yet A and B are incompatible (or even contradictory). In my view, cases of clashes between morality and ethics are usually cited as clear examples of moral dilemmas. This is not to deny that there are cases of genuine moral dilemmas, in my narrow use of the term "moral," but the force of what is usually taken as moral dilemma hinges on the clash between *morality* and *ethics*.

Sartre made famous the case of a pupil of his, a young man whose father deserted his mother, and whose elder brother was killed by the Germans in the offensive of 1940.[14] Living with his mother, being her only source of consolation in life, he faces the choice of either going to England to join the Free French Forces, or staying with his mother and helping her carry on. The young man does not doubt that he can concretely and unambiguously help his mother. He also knows that joining the general cause may end up in his performing a rather meaningless army task that will contribute nothing to the war effort, like being an army clerk or, worse, being stuck in Spain on his way to join the Free Forces.

Sartre senses that two different things are going on here, which he calls "two kinds of morality": on the one hand, the morality of sympathy and personal devotion, and on the other hand, a morality with a much wider scope but a much vaguer line of action. "He had to choose between the two."

As I read this, there are, indeed, two things going on: on the one hand, the ethical relation between son and mother; on the other hand, the moral relation of this young man to those he is supposed to help free from the inhuman Nazi occupation. We may narrow the scope of the description of joining the Free Forces by saying that all that this young man cares about is liberating the French people, with whom he has close relations. But there is no reason to assume that this is all there is to it. We can grant him that he cares about defeating the Nazis for the sake of humanity at large, and not just that he wishes to defeat Germany for the sake of helping his French people, even though helping specifically the French is part of his motivation.

Ethics (as I use the term) makes, by Sartre's account, an immediate and a concrete appeal to us, with clear yet limited consequences, whereas morality (as I use the term) has a wider appeal, but its appeal is a bit abstract and its consequences more often than not indeterminate.

Sartre's example is cited everywhere, usually in a very schematic form that shrivels what is so vivid and captivating in this example, the tension between ethics and morality. I do not want to reduce all that goes under the heading of "moral dilemmas" to the conflict between ethics and morality. Other forms of conflict routinely go under that heading; they are important forms of hard choices that concern individual compromises.

One form is the conflict between duties to oneself and duties to others. Nora in Ibsen's renowned *Doll's House* is torn between her obligations to her husband and three children and her obligations to herself. Another form is the conflict between religious obligations and strong moral and ethical obligations, Abraham's sacrifice of Isaac being a celebrated case in point.

I am concerned neither with the business of obligations to God nor with the business of obligations to oneself. Both types of obligations are not, in my use of the terms, part of morality or ethics, for morality and ethics are based on relations with other humans and not on relations with oneself or with God.

Rotten compromises can be rotten to the core, when signed, for example, for the personal gain of corrupt rulers. But rotten compromises may be the products of a conflict between ethics and morality whose outcome favors ethics, in cases where morality should have had the upper hand. A rotten compromise may be the product of a *tragic choice*. It happens in cases where one cannot reconcile morality and ethics. One is cursed by his community if one sides with morality, and cursed by humanity, in the name of morality, if one sides with one's community.

A tragic choice does not mean that there is no right answer to the dilemma. If a compromise is rotten, it means that the moral consideration should have taken the upper hand, and that there is no justification for contracting the rotten compromise. But the tragic choice means that signing a rotten compromise can be excused, not in the sense of being exonerated, but in the sense of having strong grounds for forgiveness.

In criminal law, the issue of excuse and justification wreaks havoc.[15] Some do not believe that any useful distinction can be drawn between the two, and some believe that it is terribly important to draw the distinction. The distinction that I seek is a moral one, not a legal one. Justification confers moral justification on an act ahead of its commission, whereas excuse is a rational plea for forgiveness after the act.

Any wrongdoer has the right to plead for forgiveness from the wronged side. Forgiveness is an act that expresses sovereignty on the part of the wronged side. The wronged side regains its dignity by acting like a sovereign who grants pardon or clemency to his subjects, as a gift and not as matter of right.

There must be a gratuitous element in forgiveness: without it the element of sovereignty disappears. A rational excuse is one in which there are very good reasons for the wronged side to grant forgiveness. But it should not reach the vanishing point, where forgiveness loses its nature as a gift. A rational excuse provides the wronged side with good reasons to grant forgiveness, but not compelling reasons that would make refusal to forgive irrational on the part of the wronged side.

Wrapping Up

The last two chapters are dedicated to a clause in the injunction: Thou shall not commit rotten compromise, *come what may*. The clause is the emphatic "come what may." The two chapters try to elucidate and defend the clause against various possible efforts to justify its abandonment or at least to provide mitigated circumstances that would make us give up the clause, and turn the injunction into a presumption: Do not commit rotten compromise, unless and until you have good reasons to do so.

The chapters deal with various prima facie good reasons for defending rotten compromises mostly under the generic heading of "necessity." Moreover, the two chapters provide some psychological observations as to circumstances in which people may be reluctant to accept an emphatic "come what may"—for example, circumstances of overall losses—whereas in overall gain they may be more disposed to accept the moral high ground.

The concession made for the prima facie good reasons and for the psychology and politics that go with it is that rotten compromises may be excused or understood, but they are never justified.

The upshot of the two chapters is this: the injunction should be upheld with the emphatic clause.

-6-

Sᴇᴄᴛᴀʀɪᴀɴɪꜱᴍ ᴀɴᴅ Cᴏᴍᴘʀᴏᴍɪꜱᴇ

Once Again: The Economic Picture vs. the Religious Picture of Politics

Lᴇᴛ ᴜꜱ ʀᴇᴛᴜʀɴ to our two pictures of politics: politics as economics and politics as religion.

In principle, everything in the economic picture is subject to bargaining, everything is negotiable, whereas in the religious picture centered on the idea of the holy, the holy is nonnegotiable. Commodities are divisible either physically or in terms of the duration of their use. What is divisible can be subject to compromise. We can split the difference. The sacred—at least in monotheistic religions—is the idea of that which is indivisible and hence not subject to compromise. If a fetus's life is sacred, then no splitting of pregnancy into trimesters is allowed.

The economic picture allows very little room for authority and ceremony. Authority is replaced by the relative bargaining power of the participants and the ability to enforce agreements. Ceremony is reduced to advertising, something basically manipulative and wasteful. The economic picture of politics is a mundane picture, very down-to-earth. The political protagonists look more like gray-suited accountants than like red-robed heroes or white-gowned saints.

In contrast, the religious picture of politics is dramatic. It is based on the fact that the state asks its citizens to be ready in times of war to sacrifice their lives for the state. This basic fact vitiates the economic idea that politics is merely about the satisfaction of wants. It says that politics is as much about finding the meaning of life in sacrifice. Politics as religion is a framework for giving meaning to people's lives, which goes far beyond a framework for maximizing utilities.

Most of us are in the hold of these two pictures of politics. We have a stereoscopic political perception: we recognize that some aspects of politics are better covered by one picture, while other aspects are better covered by the other. In times of war and crisis, the religious picture prevails in making sense of politics to us. In times of business as usual, the economic picture has the upper hand. Those who lack stereoscopic vision—the perception of depth that comes from the use of both eyes—look at the political world with a single eye.

Sectarianism in politics is an extreme case of viewing politics with a single eye—the eye of politics as religion. Sectarians are in the hold of the religious picture of politics, and nothing else. This does not mean that sectarians are necessarily religious. It is not necessary to be religious in order to be sectarian, but it helps.

Sectarianism is a mode of operation and a state of mind. The operation would rather split the party than split the difference. The state of mind is that of keeping your principled position uncompromised, come what may. Sectarianism is a disposition to view any compromise as a rotten compromise.

The sectarian drives the religious picture to its limit. While the religious picture is such that politics is not conducted in the spirit of compromise, it does not, however, preclude compromise on nonsacred things. The sectarian pushes this idea to the limit by viewing his position as sacred and refusing to compromise on anything. He finds compromise a sellout, a capitulation, a betrayal of the cause.

We can find a good historical example of the extreme sectarian attitude against compromise among the Khawarij ("those who go outside").[1] The sect originated during the first Islamic civil war over who should lead the Muslim community after Muhammad. This strife created the split in the Islamic world between Sunni Islam and Shi'a Islam. The third caliph, Uthman, was murdered, and a bitter struggle for succession took place between Ali, the son-in-law and cousin of the Prophet, and Muawiyah, the cousin of the murdered caliph. The Khawarij first supported Ali as the legitimate caliph. But they turned against him after the Battle of Siffin (657 CE). Since no one had the upper hand in the battle, the two sides grudgingly agreed to arbitration. That arbitration was not meant to decide the legitimate caliph, but that's the way it turned out. It was Ali's acceptance of arbitration that turned the Khawarij against him. Sacred matters are not for arbitration. The Khawarij viewed the arbitration as an act of betrayal that could not be justified by appeal to political necessity. Ultimately, they assassinated Ali. Their basic attitude was that religious compromise is always a fundamental betrayal of a principle.

There is more to the sectarian cast of mind than just a negative attitude to compromise. But in my view the refusal to compromise is its main feature. What I attempt in this chapter is to string features of sectarianism like beads on a necklace, the string being the attitude to compromise.

Note that I do not use the term "sectarian" to describe a stable character trait. I have little faith in the idea of human character. In my view one can develop a sectarian cast of mind in one situation and have an open mind in another.

Attitude to Numbers

Sects are usually small, but their ambitions are usually big, if not downright megalomaniac: nothing short of the salvation of the world. How do sects account for the disparity between the smallness of their numbers and the immensity of their ambitions? One way of dealing with that disparity is by denying the importance of numbers. Numbers don't count. There is no safety in numbers.

The Donatists were a heretical sect that prospered in the Roman part of North Africa in the fourth and fifth centuries AD. They believed that the administration of sacraments such as baptism should be performed only by holy priests. They refused to accept the authority of priests who, during that time of persecution, handed over to the Roman authorities holy books to burn.[2]

St. Augustine, representing the church, campaigned bitterly against the Donatists. Both sides to the polemics agreed that Noah's ark was an apt allegory of the church under siege. The Donatists, however, stressed the fact that Noah's ark carried only eight human beings. When the chips are down, humanity can be saved by a very small number of people. Numbers are unimportant; the quality of the people, their holiness, is all that counts. St. Augustine, in contrast, stressed the idea that in the ark there were beasts, too, and the ark was not restricted to pure creatures only. Noah's ark was a refuge to a considerable number of creatures, not just Noah's nuclear family.[3]

The sectarians do not worship Atlas. They do not hold that one heroic creature can shoulder the whole weight of the world, but they come close. A small group can indeed, like Atlas, prevent the sky from falling and crushing the earth. It is an assignment not for one hero, but for a small group of the elect.

Sectarians diverge in their attitudes toward small numbers. There are *avant-garde* sectarians, and there are *remnant* sectarians. According to the avant-garde approach, finding a new path in an unexplored terrain calls for a small vanguard of skilled and dedicated people to lead the advancing masses of the future. Similarly, in an army operation, the unit that reconnoiters the way is small; the big army advances later. According to the remnant approach, only a few will survive the cataclysmic events in store for humanity, and the future of the world depends on them. Noah's ark is an expression of the remnant approach.

The sectarians' disregard for numbers makes them unwilling to compromise. You do not compromise for the sake of vague political recruitment, since that is unimportant if numbers do not count. Thus the dilution of one's cause through compromise for the sake of recruitment debases the cause. It makes that cause not worth fighting for.

Sects can be internally democratic; their members may strongly believe in equality among the initiated. But the general attitude of sectarians is undemocratic on several counts: in their elitist attitude to outsiders, in their hostile attitude to compromise, and in their disregard of numbers. In democracy, numbers count and are counted. As for compromise, it breathes life into democracy: democracy calls for constantly forming coalitions. No compromise, no coalition.

I should qualify my hasty claim that sectarians disregard numbers. Their attitude can be more complicated than a mere disregard of numbers. What counts is the numbers of future generations. The attitude, of course, varies from sect to sect. Some sectarians, especially the sectarians of the Left, believe that the masses are in principle on their side, but that they cannot express themselves as yet, either because they are oppressed or because they are deluded by the manipulations of their exploiters. Such sectarians maintain that they are a minority, but only temporarily. To ensure that future masses flock to the present heresy of the sectarians and make it the orthodoxy of tomorrow, the message should not be dimmed by any compromise. The creed of the sect is heresy. The creed of the church, of the establishment in general, is orthodoxy. What passes as orthodoxy and what passes as heresy, much like what counts as language and what counts as dialect, depends on who is in power, but it also depends on numbers. The sectarian believes that the heresy of today is the orthodoxy of tomorrow. But this will happen by massive conversion, not by messy compromise.

Narcissism of Minor Differences

Once upon a time there were two good friends, Piet Mondrian and Theo van Doesburg. Mondrian, the elder of the two, took the lead. Van Doesburg converted to Mondrian's way of painting, becoming his friend and disciple. Then, in 1924, when they were together in Paris, they split. The reason for the split is still debated among art historians, but by one account, which I find too good to be false, van Doesburg did the heretical thing: he started painting in diagonal lines rather than in the strict horizontal lines of Mondrian. This was quite enough to cause a split from which two artistic visions emerged: Elementalism, as van Doesburg called his diagonal approach, and Neo-Plasticism, as Mondrian dubbed his own approach.[4]

To outsiders, the difference between horizontal Mondrians and diagonal van Doesburgs looks minor. To Mondrian, it looked like all the difference in the world. He held van Doesburg responsible, by his act of diagonal hubris, for destroying the cosmic order, knocking it off its delicate balance.

I take the story of the split between Mondrian and van Doesburg as a parable for sectarianism and its concern with minor differences. Freud coined the expression "narcissism of minor differences," a particularly felicitous expression to describe the cast of mind of the sectarian. Freud applied the narcissism of minor differences to groups as well as to individuals. Viewing differences as minor is not a symmetrical relation. Seymour Lipset made the point that differences viewed as minor from the perspective of the United States are not regarded as minor by Canadians. For one thing, the identity of Canadians hinges on such differences, and identity is no minor matter.[5]

Sectarianism is the tendency to inflate a minor disagreement over beliefs, or practices, until it becomes impossible for the sectarians and those not of their party to live together. The sectarian behaves like a social amoeba: even when there is only one cell, it manages to split itself. In an adverse environment the sectarian-like amoeba tends to become a cyst, isolating itself totally from the outside world in order to stay alive.

The relation between the narcissism of small differences and a negative attitude toward compromise is rather straightforward. If the differences are objectively minor, there is very little room for compromise since there is not enough difference to split the difference. This is one of the reasons why civil wars are so bitter in comparison to wars between states. I shall come to civil wars later.

Manichaeism

The sectarian mind tends to be Manichaean. It has a strong sense of dualism—between the realm of light and goodness (us) and the realm of darkness and evil (them). Some of the outstanding sects may have been Manichaean in the literal sense, namely, those under the influence of the dualistic religion Manichaeism, started by the prophet Mani in the third century. I have in mind Paulicianism in Armenia and Anatolia between the seventh and ninth centuries, Bogomilism in Bulgaria from the tenth century until much later, and Catharism in the Languedoc region of France between the eleventh and thirteenth centuries. All upheld the dualism of the autonomous realms of good and evil. Manichaeism in all its forms was taken as heretical, undermining the idea of God as the creator of all there is.

My interest in the sectarian cast of mind is general, not directed to the strict metaphysical view of the dualism of good and evil. I am interested in what I shall call practical Manichaeism, that is, viewing the world as in fact being divided between the good "us" and the evil "them"—the axis of evil, if you like. Indeed, the Manichaean worldview does not divide the world simply between light and darkness but rather between blazing light and pitch darkness. There is no twilight zone, no room for compromise: it is "either-or."

If there ever was a sect that manifested the sectarian mind to perfection, it was the Dead Sea sect (otherwise known as the Qumran sect or the Essenes). The Dead Sea sect is clearly a sect, and its writings clearly heterodoxy, yet Edna Ullmann-Margalit is right in arguing in her book *Out of the Cave* that there is no clear church and no clear orthodoxy that the sect and its writings can be contrasted with.[6]

One of the Dead Sea sectarian scrolls is about the apocalyptic war, "The War between the Sons of Light and the Sons of Darkness," a war that the sectarians imagine taking part in. The sectarian mind has a siege mentality, always caught in a war between the sons of light and the sons of darkness.

It is not a mere war; at the end of the day, it is a permanent war. The crucial battle, Armageddon, may take place at the end of days, but the war is continuous. The sectarians are on guard. They are constantly morally ambushing their sectarian comrades to see who is going to betray the cause and join the children of darkness. Moral ambush is indeed the hallmark of the sectarian, who incessantly looks for signs of deviations, of not having the correct view about everything. A readiness to compromise is the first sign the ambushing sectarians look for, an unfailing sign of those about to betray.

Even the Amish with their proverbial capacity for forgiveness would cite as a pillar of their way of life the verse "Be not yoked with unbelievers. For what do righteousness and wickedness have in common? Or what fellowship can light have with darkness?" (2 Corinthians 6:14).

Sectarian Manichaeism may take a milder form. The sectarian claims a monopoly on all values. There is no good value outside the sect. But outsiders can still be of instrumental value to the sect. Secular Jews in the eyes of most ultraorthodox sectarians have no values whatsoever, but they may have instrumental value if their tax money is channeled into the ultraorthodox community.

The revolutionary party monopolizes all the values. But on occasion the party forms a front with so-called progressive elements to gain power. The progressives are instrumentally valuable for their potential willingness to be a front for the party. But such an alliance is tentative and puts a strain on its more sectarian members, who are strictly Manichaean—for example, those who believed there was no difference between the Social Democrats of the Weimar Republic and the Nazis. This brings us to a related feature of the Manichaean worldview of the sectarian, the obsession with purity.

Purity and Corruption

The Dead Sea sect is paradigmatic in its obsession with ritual purity. The number of ritual baths in the arid compound of the Essenes near the Dead Sea is staggering. So are their manuals of purity. Sectarians are indeed obsessed with purity, be it ritual cleanliness, innocent freedom from evil and guilt, chastity, purity of doctrine, or even purity of language. Puritans were worried about cursing God. Politically correct Puritans are worried about cursing minorities.

One powerful idea associated with the notion of the holy is that of being subject to restrictions. The restrictions are meant to protect the Divine from human pollution and to protect humans from the dangerous presence of the Divine—to shield them from the Divine by purity. The administration of the holy is very much on the religious sectarian mind. To administer restrictive practices and taboos is essential to religious sects.

The religious idea of purity and taboo invades politics, sometimes to good effect. For example, Thomas Schelling keeps reminding us that the taboo on the use of nuclear weapons has protected us so far.[7] It is thanks to the taboo rather than to utilitarian calculations of profit and loss that these weapons are not deployed. Nuclear weapons are taken as the ultimate polluter, and so they should be. There is, of course, a pernicious consequence to the idea of purity, the idea of racial purity.

Purity is based not so much on the idea of putting things in their proper place as on the fear of mixing categories. The categories most in need of being kept apart are the sacred and the profane. But the categories of sacredness for different religions should also be kept apart. The sectarian mind, obsessed with purity in one form or another, regards compromise as an act of pollution. Compromise is negotiating with those who are stained, and thus it involves mixing categories. Having two religions—say, the ones already mentioned, Hinduism and Islam—sharing what for Hindus is the birthplace of Rama and for Muslims the Mosque of Babur, is mixing categories, much as with Jews and Muslims sharing what for Jews is the Temple Mount and for Muslims the Noble Sanctuary. The sense of mixing categories may be experienced by ordinary believers of those religions, but for the sectarians of Vishwa Hindu Parishad (VHP), or for the Jewish Loyalists of the Temple Mount, entertaining the thought of compromise, let alone negotiation, is anathema.

In general, the sectarian is in favor of purging and splitting for the sake of retaining the integrity of what should be kept pure. Shit is the negation of the pure. The sectarian craves life without shit. Compromise is part and parcel of the shitty world.

Related to the sectarian idea of purity is its correlate—the idea that the world around the sectarian is thoroughly corrupt and corrupting. This may mean *metaphysical corruption* and it may mean *human corruption* (personal or institutional); quite often it means both. Many sects hold the world to be metaphysically corrupt; in their view, the fact that the material world is subject to decay and rot is of great moment. The material world is corrupt; by contrast, the spiritual world is eternal and never rots.

The corrupt nature of the material world is sometimes blamed on humanity, "the Fall," and sometimes, as in the Gnostic case, on an evil god. Sects that hold the world to be metaphysically corrupt tend to cut themselves off from the material world, so as to live the pure life of the spirit. They view materialistic life as compromising one's life in a most fundamental way (compromising in the sense of reducing greatly the value of one's life).

The sectarian usually has a strong sense of living in a corrupt society from which one should keep apart. The sectarian is an avid collector of signs of corruption. Compromise is for the sectarian such a sign: a sign of duplicity, sleaze, and treachery—all these and more the sectarian associates with the very spirit of compromise.

Sects and Secrets

The sectarian attitude to compromise is hostile. But sects in general are minorities in a hostile environment. Some sects are actively persecuted. Others have good reasons to fear persecution. Though sects may value martyrdom as the highest religious fulfillment, not all sects require a proclamation of faith in the face of serious harm. Sects, especially sects with a history of persecution, develop techniques of survival meant to shield the believers. The famous Islamic doctrine of dissimulation (*takiyya*), which became identified mainly with Shi'a Islam, is a clear example. In time of potential danger it allows the believers to dissimulate their true beliefs in their overt behavior and utterances. They must, however, keep their true beliefs in their hearts.[8]

The compromise involved in *takiyya* is not the kind of voluntary agreement of mutual concession that we are discussing, but it is compromise nonetheless: the compromising of one's religious principles in the face of possible harm.

Calculating the possible harm that justifies dissimulation is indeed part of the considerations of different sects. Thus the Ismaili, the second largest branch of Shi'a, is known to have developed a rather sophisticated calculus to assess the probability of danger that justifies *takiyya*. The point, however, is that even sects with a strong sense of straightforwardness and a strong reluctance toward dissimulation, such as Ibadism, a distinct sect of Islam, are committed to the doctrine of *takiyya*, viewing it as the garb of the believer necessary for maintaining one's religion in a hostile world.

Another justification of dissimulation is found in the Catholic Church under the doctrine of *accommodation*, a doctrine strongly associated with the Jesuits.[9] Accommodation started as a hermeneutic doctrine of adapting the wording of a text in changing circumstances. But it moved far beyond. We can judge how far if we consider the behavior of two famous Jesuit missionaries to China in the sixteen century: Matteo Ricci and Michele Ruggieri. They accommodated God to the Confucian Heaven (*t'ien*). Indeed, the Jesuits were accused by their critics, Catholic and Protestant alike, of being dissimulators and prone to conspiracy. The term "Jesuitical" in English acquired the sense of equivocation. The Jesuits are an order, not a sect, but the history of the order, especially in the periods of banishment from various Catholic countries, has many sectarian features, at least in the eyes of its critics.

The point I am making is that although sects and sectarians are strong advocates of purity, they are far from advocating transparency. There are two related reasons for that. One just mentioned is that, historically, sects were persecuted or were in constant danger of being persecuted. Thus many sects adopted concealment as a mode of survival, which in turn gave rise to deep suspicions that sects were secret societies endangering the body politic. A strange dialectics took place within sects. Sectarians everywhere accuse orthodoxy of being organized hypocrisy, yet they themselves are forced to conceal their own beliefs and practices, thereby drawing upon their own members the accusation of hypocrisy.

The second reason for lack of transparency among sectarians has to do with the sectarians' reading of canonical texts.

They read them as coded messages clear only to the elite members of the sect (all or some). The reading deviates from the overt standard orthodox interpretation. The orthodoxy is accused of corrupting the true meaning of the canonical texts, and in turn it accuses the sect's reading of heresy. This is familiar to the point of banality.

The esoteric tendencies of the sectarians lead them to believe that nothing is what it appears and that everything important is hidden. Paying attention to outward interpretations is being superficial. The truth is hidden deep, never on the surface.

These esoteric tendencies also lead sectarians not only to elitism but also to hierarchy—not everyone can be trusted with the secret reading, not even members of the sect who are, as yet, uninitiated. The more secretive the sect is, the more we can expect it to be hierarchical, and hence less democratic. Newcomers are never trusted with the deep secrets. The members of the sect become privy to the secrets by degree. The degree of access to the secrets depends on the member's rank in the hierarchy.

Moshe Halbertal, who masterfully treats the subject of esotericism in religion and politics, finds an intimate relation between esoteric tendencies and the tendency to use conspiracy theories extensively.[10] Particle physicists believe that the true reality is hidden, but they do not believe that the world hides it on purpose. Sectarian esotericism usually holds that the world truth is hidden intentionally. The world is governed by grand conspiracy. The sectarians believe that they have decoded a redemptive scheme to enable them to overcome evil conspiracies based on secret agreements among evil forces that prevent the world from being run justly. Gnostic sects are a typical example of this way of thinking; but they are not alone. Secular sectarians, who believe that they have decoded a redemptive scheme of historical laws, believe also that those on the wrong end of the redemptive scheme, the losers in the historical progress, will do everything in their power to prevent the march of history, and constantly conspire against the forces of progress. The conspirators run the world now—not in the future. Any compromise with the existing order is tantamount to collaborating with those forces that are on the wrong side of history.

Radical sectarians believe that liberals are acting in Jesuitical ways, changing their color like chameleons, hiding their manipulative interests in the name of tolerance and pluralism. Once the liberals' cherished interests are endangered, they bare their claws.

The sectarian spots a disparity between the liberal ideology advocating transparency, on the one hand, and the liberal rulers finding transparency an obnoxious obstruction, on the other hand. Transparency exposes the rulers to criticism they do not like; it demystifies their claims to superior knowledge and superior judgment, and reveals them as vulnerable human beings. They sense that it detracts from their ability to rule.

Indeed transparency is an obstacle to making shady, shoddy, and shabby agreements. More important, it makes it harder to sign rotten agreements. Secret agreements, or secret addenda to open agreements, are usually where the dirty stuff conjures its mischief. Even regimes not attuned to public opinion, like Nazi Germany and the Soviet Union, needed a secret protocol included in their overt Molotov-Ribbentrop agreements, and for years and years the Soviet Union denied the existence of such a protocol. It was not until December 1989 that the newly democratically elected Soviet Congress of the People passed a resolution admitting the existence of secret protocols and condemning them.

Not all sectarians hold their beliefs to be esoteric. Some feel that they are transparent and obvious.

The sectarian mind has a particular attitude to error. The ones who are in the wrong are not merely mistaken; they are evil. They deny the truth out of corruption and not out of distorted cognition. It is because of the truth's transparent and obvious nature that the explanation for its denial should be found not in cognition but in the resolve. The ill will on the part of those in error prevents them from seeing the light. They have ill will, and they are not merely ill-informed. Their errors are sinful, since their lives are based on wicked moral beliefs; they are more than mistaken—they are sinners who deserve hate. Sectarians are haters. They hate not just the error but the ones who err. For the sectarian there are no immaculate preconceptions, only original sinners.

There is a brand of sectarianism which believes that the truth is for anyone—anyone with purity of heart. Nothing is really hidden. The reason why others deny the obvious is because they are stiff-necked, clinging to their old beliefs because they are rotten to the core.

Sectarianism and Sectorialism

I was raised in a sectorial society, a society divided into different sectors. The sector I belonged to was the labor movement sector. Prestate Israel was sectorial through and through, from its early days. There was the civil sector, which my parents called the bourgeois sector, and then the religious sector and the ultrareligious sector. The dominant one, however, was the labor sector. These sectors were further subdivided. The newspapers we read at home belonged to our sector; the school I went to belonged to our sector; the youth movement, the sports clubs, our songs and holidays were shaped by the sector; our neighborhood, our dress, indeed our outfits were sectorial, and so were the theater, the cinema, and the restaurant. All the functions normally provided by a welfare state, such as health and education, were provided by sectors.[11]

In short, every aspect of life was covered by the sector. There were some stylistic variations within sectors owing to their subdivisions, but, for the most part, the sectors were all-encompassing. When the need arose to form a national soccer squad, the labor teams sent five Hapoel players, the civil sector sent five Maccabi players, and the ultranationalists sent one Betar player. Two brothers from Betar deserved to be on the team but they had to spell one another because their sector was allocated only one player. Sectorial society is based first and foremost on belonging; achievements come after.

I can easily imagine that the reality I depict does not differ materially from the reality of the chariot races in Byzantium (circa 532 CE) when the Blues and the Greens were not just two competing teams but two package deals.[12] The package consisted, among other things, of their views on the nature of the godhead. Is it one nature (the Monophysite Green team), or is it two natures (the Chalcedonian Blue team)? Perhaps the Protestant Rangers and the Catholic Celtics in Scotland are not merely two soccer teams but also two packages of that weird kind.

Each sector in the sectorial society of my childhood had a total vision of what was good for the whole society. The sectorial society was a competition between those visions of society as manifested by their different ways of life. One thing, however, prevented the sectorial society of my youth from deteriorating into sectarian violence. There was a deep commitment to live together. It was based on some vague but strong sense of Jewish solidarity and, for most sectors, as well on the unifying theme of Zionism, the creation of a national homeland for all Jews.

Both the sectarians and the sectorialists deal with the world on a wholesale basis. Their views and practices form a package deal: take it or leave it. This is in contrast to the economic picture of politics, where we deal with the world on a retail basis: many deals can be made, and we don't just take it or leave it.

Yet the sectorialist, unlike the sectarian, has an overriding commitment to keeping a shared framework. This commitment calls for some compromises that the sectorialist would grudgingly accept but that the sectarian would reject. The sectarians do not feel the force of the need to compromise, just for the sake of sharing life with those who disagree with them. They may be coerced to share a public space with others. But coercion is not compromise.

The sectorialists, unlike the sectarians, care about numbers. They try to convert society and shape it in the mold of their sector. Caring about numbers makes one open to compromise. In any case, sectorial movements feel responsible for their constituency, and this leads them to seek compromises, even against their very instincts. Movements like the Palestinian Hamas, the Lebanese Hezbollah, and the Israeli Sephardic Shas are sectorial rather than sectarian movements.[13] But in times of crisis brought about by weak and corrupt governments, sectorial movements turn sectarian.

A Sectarian War

Since the Second World War, five times as many civil wars as wars between states have taken place. Those wars are very bitter. An interstate war lasts on average less than three months, while a civil war lasts on average about six years. The total number of people killed in civil wars is about five times the casualty rate of interstate wars.[14]

Some civil wars are labeled sectarian wars, such as the civil war between Protestants and Catholics in Northern Ireland, between Greek Cypriots and Turkish Cypriots, and between Shiites and Sunnis in Iraq. Those are paradigmatic cases of sectarian civil wars.

Every sectarian war is a civil war, but not every civil war is a sectarian war. We call a war sectarian if and only if there is a religious dimension to the warring groups. This does not mean that a sectarian war is necessarily about religion. It means, however, that the sides of the conflict identify themselves by religious labels. My claim is that what is important for understanding civil wars is not so much whether a conflict is about religion, as whether the sides to the conflict are in the clutch of the religious picture of politics.

Thucydides was perhaps the first historian to try to give an account of the conditions for a civil war—*stasis*. He viewed civil war with the horror it deserves. What Thucydides found so horrendous and puzzling about civil war is that it is a breakdown of an organic political unit, the Hellenic city-state, the *polis*.[15] The puzzle was how bitterly it is fought. The internal strife he had in mind as a model for all civil wars occurred in the fourth year of the Peloponnesian War (427 BC), in Corcyra. It was characterized by mutual slaughter, despicable acts of betrayal, defilement of religious sanctuaries, and utter lawlessness. Since he viewed civil war as something taking place in what is supposedly an organic political unit, he regarded civil war in medical terms as a disease. A healthy organism lives in harmony. Thucydides' main observation is that civil war usually takes place in the context of an external war, like the Peloponnesian War.

An external war may put so much pressure on organic political units that they break apart. If I may be forgiven the anachronism, Thucydides would have identified the American war in Iraq as the main cause of the Iraqi civil war. On the other hand, he wouldn't have regarded Iraq as an "organic" political entity. But then no political entity is truly organic. The organic picture of politics is influenced by a religious myth. The idea that the church is the body of Christ (Corpus Christi) is an expression of this idea.

Some Recent Lessons: Fraternal War

A civil war within a community of believers is a terrible religious sin. This is the Islamic notion of *fitna* (internal strife) within the *umma* (the community of believers). The first Islamic civil war that brought about the split between Shiites and Sunnis counts as the first and the greatest *fitna*. Among Muslims, especially Sunnis, Islamic *fitna* is the ultimate religious horror: it is viewed as sectarianism gone wild.[16]

Many Palestinians regard the current split in the Palestinian community between Hamas and Fatah as a tragic case of *fitna*.[17] They share Thucydides' view of the causes of the current *fitna*, namely, the Israeli external war against the Palestinians, but the internal strife is viewed by both sides as *fitna*, each side blaming the other for bringing about this religious sin. The current Palestinian *fitna* is accompanied by a parallel fear of civil war among the Jews in Israel, if a compromise with the Palestinians is reached. If Muslims view with horror the first Islamic *fitna*, Jews view with horror the internal war waged by their zealots, as when they were under Roman siege in the year 70 (CE). Jews call such internal strife *milkhemet ahkheim*, fraternal war.

The ideological Jewish settlers in the occupied territories vacillate between two positions: sectorialism and sectarianism. The test case is what the settlers will do if the government, backed by a parliamentary majority, decides to evacuate the settlements—all or most—within the framework of an agreement with the Palestinians. Will the settlers opt for civil war, fighting the decision by force, or will they just protest loudly? The sectorialists will vehemently protest but will not fight. They are committed to an overarching principle of living together, and they will shy away from using live ammunition in a confrontation with the majority. The sectarians, for their part, are determined to resist evacuation at all costs, and are ready to risk an internal war.

At the time of the evacuation of the Gaza Strip settlements, the sectorialists had the upper hand. But the West Bank is not Gaza, and among the young ideological settlers the sectarian zealots seem to gather momentum. Sectorialists and sectarians alike want everyone to believe that they are ready for civil war, so that the Center in Israel will give in. They believe that most Israelis who might mildly support an agreement with the Palestinians will refrain from supporting it if the price is internal strife. They believe that the majority of Jews prefer conflict between Jews and Arabs to that between Jews and Jews. Sectorialists and sectarians among the Jewish settlers share the belief that if they convey to the rest of society their readiness to fight with force, the majority of Jews in Israel will refrain from confronting them.

The current effort to reach an agreement between Israel and the Palestinians is squeezed between the fear of a Palestinian *fitna*, whereby Hamas may veto an agreement with Israel, and Israeli fear of a fraternal war, whereby the settlers may also veto an agreement. To believe that, in this situation, compromise is within reach calls for a great leap of faith.

The question whether the settlers, on the whole, will be sectarians or sectorialists, much like the question whether Hamas will be sectarian or sectorial, is of vital importance for the future of an eventual compromise, but only time will tell.

The Other Pole: The Liberal Mind and the Mind of a Social Democrat

For the liberal mind, the spirit of compromise is what should breathe life into politics. The spirit of compromise infuses compromise with a strong sense of recognition of others' values and interests. It converges with the spirit of tolerance toward objectionable beliefs and behavior.

So compromise and tolerance are for the liberal mind two sides of the same coin, and the icon of the liberal should be minted on both sides.

Tolerance and, with it, compromise, seem to be deeply puzzling. We were all taught in elementary logic class that ad hominem argument is a paradigm of fallaciousness. The scheme of such fallacious argument is painfully familiar.

If A makes the claim p, and there is something wrong with A, we infer that p is false. It seems that in being tolerant, one commits the reverse of an ad hominem fallacy.

In the reverse ad hominem fallacy: A makes the claim p that we believe to be false. However, there is something right about A. So we infer that there should be something right about p.

From our desire to recognize A, we come to recognize A's claim as a reason for us to accommodate our behavior, even though we believe that A's claim, judged on its merit, is a bad reason or no reason.

Put differently, in trying to be positive about the claim maker (the hominem) we partly accept something that we believe we should reject.

If ad hominem argument is invalid insofar as it addresses the one who makes the claim rather than the substance of the claim, the same holds true in the case of toleration and compromise.

Given the puzzling nature of compromise out of tolerance, the enemy of the liberal is quick to use two opposite tools from its polemic kit against the liberal. With one tool—addressing the spirit of compromise out of tolerance—the liberal is attacked by the enemy for lacking all conviction, and for readiness to dilute every position for the sake of accommodation. The liberal is a sheep in sheep's clothing. With the other tool, the liberal is attacked for being just another type of sectarian. This tool recasts the liberal as one who subversively promotes the spirit of compromise so as to impose her doctrine of a neutral public space: a space in which there is no room for the concept of the good, and in particular no room for religious ideas of the good life. The liberal is a secular sectarian wolf in sheep's clothing.

A polemic kit usually consists not so much of lies as of half truths. The idea is that two half truths, when directed to a worthy enemy, add up to one big truth. Thus, for example, a polemic kit against the Jews used these two tools: they are responsible for bringing about capitalism, and they are also responsible for bringing about communism. As with the accusations of the Jews, the two accusations against the liberal are two half truths rather than total falsities: one half truth is that the liberal lacks all convictions; the other is that the liberal is full of disguised convictions.

If the liberal postures as the opposite of the sectarian, the social democrat stands next to him. By a social democrat I mean a believer in forcing government, by democratic means, to steer a people to form an increasingly just society.

Can a social democrat be sectarian? Can a social democrat be a sectorialist? My short answer to the first question is no. My short answer to the second is, it depends. Unfortunately, the short answers do not help much.

It is quite obvious that the ideal type of a social democrat (say, a composite of Hjalmar Branting of Sweden, Jean Jaurès of France, and Hugh Gaitskell of Britain) is the negative of the sectarian mind. All the features I mentioned as typifying the sectarian mind would be negated by the ideal social democrat: the elitist disregard for numbers, the Manichaean vision of the world, the narcissism of minor differences—and add to that one more distinctive feature, the attitude toward *mistakes.*

With the picture of politics as religion comes the view that mistakes in politics are sinful. They are never just cognitive failures. The sectarian tends to regard the mistakes of his enemy as mortal sins. There is a redeeming feature in the religious thought and sensibility about sinful error, the idea of the frailty of human beings. The sectarian takes from the religious picture the idea of sinful error, but he is not attuned to the accompanying idea, namely, the idea of human vulnerability. In the sectarian's view a mistaken sinner is not a fallen man but a fallen angel—a demon.

In the economic picture of politics, one has to pay for the mistakes one commits. But mistakes are not transgression of higher commands (whether commands of God or the command of history). Mistakes are cognitive failures, not moral failures. There is very little room for compassion toward the mistaken ones in the economic picture, but there is also very little possibility of considering them as transgressors of the higher realms. The sectarians take the unfortunate features of both pictures and end up viewing mistakes as sins that do not call for compassion. They turn every venial sin into a mortal one.

Social democracy works by trial and error rather than by following a doctrinal blueprint. So error is viewed as an essential by-product of social democracy. Social democracy is committed to tolerating mistakes. Mistakes are not grounds for banishment, ostracism, and denunciation; only in extreme cases are they grounds for a split. The idea of social democracy is an open society, which means a society in which alternative ways of life are not only tolerated but appreciated, even when regarded as partially mistaken. An open society has an intrinsic relation to the idea of alternatives. In a closed society there is no room for alternatives, be they alternative ways of life, alternative views, or alternative policies. A closed society can be closed by the yoke of tradition, by police brutality, by a sectarian cast of mind, or by a combination of any of the above. It rejects alternatives with the justification that with alternatives errors creep in. So in addition to the features I mentioned typical of the sectarian mind and not of the social democrat's, we should add an attitude toward mistakes as an important new way to distinguish them.

What about the social democrats' attitude to compromise? How do they fare compared to the sectarians in their hostility to compromise?

Historically social democrats' attitude to compromise has been misleading. Social democrats joined bourgeois politics in the belief that it is possible both, in the short run, to improve workers' conditions by political means and, in the long run, to bring about socialism through secured ballots rather than through sprays of bullets.

Social democrats, in contrast to revolutionary socialists, used to believe that in the long run they are bound overwhelmingly to win elections. So much so that they conveniently accepted Marx's mistaken prognosis that in capitalism, the middle class is bound to disappear, the working class will swell numerically, and the ranks of capitalists will shrink to insignificance. For a while it looked that way. In the heyday of social democratic parties, they expanded phenomenally within a very short time. Thus, for example, the German SPD grew from 120,000 votes in 1875 to 4,250,000 on the eve of World War I. In 1890, it was already the largest party in Germany.[18]

So the belief that the future was destined to be socialist by democratic means had a basis in fact. The capitalists would, of course, resist any structural change in capitalism, but since there were too few of them to resist the pressure, they would all be swept away by the fated majority. As it turned out, this hope was not fulfilled. The working class has shrunk in developed countries, and social democratic parties have become increasingly divorced from their working-class base, since that base was so much smaller.

At their peak, social democratic parties moved on a fast sectorial track. The idea was that social democrats' parties and workers' unions would create a separate form of life within the bourgeois state, without the taint of bourgeois characteristics. This, they believed, would enable the social democrats to retain their long-run commitment to a radical change toward socialism. Thus a division was created between the short-run goals of improving workers' conditions, which called for a great deal of compromise, and the long-run goal of socialism, which left no room for compromise, apart from the commitment to achieve it by democratic means.

My claim is that historically social democracy started as a sectorialist movement. No one in the movement was allowed to say it out loud, since the working class regarded itself as a universal class that stood for the liberation of humanity at large, but it was sectorialist through and through, whether it admitted it or not. All this changed utterly when social democratic parties joined bourgeois governments, either as junior partners or as leading partners. They joined for lots of reasons, the most compelling being the need to compromise with the middle class because their own class base was shrinking.

In competing for the hearts and minds of the middle class, the social democrats started speaking for "the nation" rather than for the working class. It was Ben-Gurion, the leader of the Labor Party in Israel, who coined the slogan "From class to nation." This slogan says it all.

Sectorialism stopped being an option for social democrats; their working-class base became too narrow to win elections. They needed, and still need, allies among the middle class, which means the end of the sectorialist option.

So here is my conclusion. Sectarianism is utterly incompatible with social democracy: for the social democrats, sectarianism is not just "a waste" but the opposite of what they stand for. And sectorialism, once historically and conceptually compatible with social democracy, is no longer a viable option. What it means is that the social democrat, like the liberal, should adopt the spirit of compromise, out of necessity, if not out of principle.

CONCLUSION
BETWEEN EVIL AND RADICAL EVIL

✹

FROM THE REALITY of recent sectarian wars and civil wars, we return to the formative event of the Second World War and its antecedents. The issue is simple. If having an agreement with Hitler in Munich was rotten, was it also rotten to side with Stalin against Hitler?

Note that siding with one rotten regime against an aggressor, as in the case of Nazi Germany invading the Soviet Union, is not exactly signing an agreement that can technically be rendered rotten. It was not a compromise: it was collaboration against a common enemy, which was unmistakably the aggressor. However, the decision to side with one rotten regime against the other raises questions that bear directly on the issue of the nature of rotten compromises. So I shall treat the issue of siding with the Soviet Union as an issue about rotten compromise, acknowledging that it is not technically so.

"The Russian Revolution and the National Socialist ascendancy in Germany are the two most important sources of evidence of moral philosophy in our time, as the French Revolution was for Hegel and Marx, and later to Tocqueville and for Mill. Although both revolutions produced, both in intention and in effect, a triumph on a gigantic scale, there are often marked differences between the evil effects planned and achieved."[1] This observation comes from Stuart Hampshire, a keen philosophical connoisseur of the twentieth century.

It is embarrassingly banal to say that these two historical events shook the world. But it is less banal, although true, to say that they created a change in the world order which in turn resulted in grave moral consequences. Both paved the way to unparalleled murderous regimes (especially if we view Mao's regime as connected, however indirectly, to the October Revolution).

It is injustice, not justice, that brings us into normative politics—despotism, not freedom. Moral political theory should start with negative politics, the politics that informs us on how to tackle evil before telling us how to pursue the good. Stalin's communism and Hitler's Nazism are perhaps the most glaringly dark examples, if I may be allowed the oxymoron, of evil. Thus negative moral politics should be informed by these two examples and should be able to provide us with the moral vocabulary adequate for coping with them. Indeed the way we judge these two examples, and especially the way we compare them, is a test case of how adequate our moral account is. This, in any case, is how I understand Stuart Hampshire's opening statement.

Morality, like wine tasting, calls for constant comparative judgments. Possibly, as Gilbert Ryle perhaps thought, as in the case of wine tasting, there is not much theory involved in morality, but only subtle variations of comparative judgments.[2] If a theory is to emerge from the efforts to make such comparative judgments coherent, it may be a little theory, not a grand one.

One crucial comparative judgment that tests such a moral theory and gives us a taste for it is the moral comparison identifying the lesser evil between Stalin's communism and Hitler's Nazism. Note that I do not submit for comparison generic communism and generic fascism. I do not offer, say, Pol Pot compared to Generalissimo Franco. Already the moral comparison between the regimes of Hitler and Stalin is burdened with the fact that Hitler ruled for twelve years whereas Stalin ruled twice as long. What does that double span mean? Should we compare what Stalin actually did to what Hitler would have done, had he remained in power as long as Stalin did, or should we compare Stalin's deeds just to Hitler's actual deeds? I shall compare only facts to facts, and not facts to counterfactuals. So I shall compare Stalin's actual ruling to Hitler's actual ruling, even though we can easily imagine the moral havoc Hitler would have inflicted, had he ruled for double the time he actually did. But one thing is clear: the comparison between Stalin's regime and Hitler's regime is more focused and more confined and defined in space and time than is the general comparison between generic communism and generic fascism.

Churchill's Judgment

On June 21, 1941, at a dinner at Chequers, Churchill stated that Hitler was planning to attack Russia, relying on right-wing sympathies in Britain and the United States not to allow their governments to interfere. But Hitler is wrong, Churchill stated, and Britain will help Russia. After dinner, the issue of helping Russia came up again. Mr. Colville, Churchill's private secretary, asked him how he, Churchill, the arch anti-communist, could support Russia. Doesn't this support for Russia, he asked, amount to "bowing down in the House of Rimmon" (meaning, compromising his principles).[3]?

Churchill's secretary alluded to the Aramaic military commander Na'aman who, after being cured of leprosy by the prophet Elijah, promised to worship God alone. But then, as an afterthought, Na'aman asked that he be excused in those cases when he had to follow his master, the earthly king, and bow down to the Aramaic idol Rimmon. The prophet granted this request. Hence, in the biblical sense, bowing down in the House of Rimmon is recognized as a necessary compromise, not to be reproached.

This, in any case, is how I understand the question that Churchill was asked. His reply is vintage Churchill: "Not at all. I have only one purpose; the destruction of Hitler, and my life is much simplified thereby. If Hitler invaded Hell, I would make at least a favorable reference to the Devil in the House of Commons."[4]

The following day Churchill went on the air. In his speech he compared the two regimes. "The Nazi regime is indistinguishable from the worst features of Communism. It is devoid of all theme and principle except appetite and racial domination. It excels all forms of human wickedness in the efficiency of its cruelty and ferocious aggression. No one has been a more consistent opponent of Communism than I have for the last twenty-five years. I will unsay no word that I have spoken about it. But all this fades away before the spectacle which is now unfolding. The past, with its crimes, its follies, and its tragedies, flashes away."[5] And then he went on to remark favorably on the devil Stalin. I believe that Churchill made the right moral choice in siding with Stalin against Hitler. This, I maintain, is true even according to our retrospective knowledge of Stalin's crimes, the extent of which presumably was unknown to Churchill.

There is no question that Stalin's worst crimes were committed in the years before the war, and that Hitler's worst crimes were committed during the war. When Churchill made his judgment, Stalin had already committed his worst, whereas Hitler was far from having done his worst yet. And yet I believe Churchill was right, not because Stalin's worst was not up to Hitler's worse-than-worst, but because Hitler's evil was radical evil, undermining morality itself. Stalin's monstrous evil was different, and Churchill correctly sensed the difference when he said that Hitler stands for one thing: "racial domination." This is what I shall argue.

One may wonder whether my understanding of Churchill's choice is not an exercise in misguided moralism. This argument sees Churchill as having made a political judgment, not a moral one: he deemed Hitler more dangerous than Stalin to Britain and to the British Empire. I do not think so. Churchill obviously was concerned with the interests of Britain, as he understood them. And it is true that he judged Stalin less dangerous than Hitler, not just because Stalin in foreign affairs was the devil he knew whereas Hitler was the new devil. But Stalin's crimes were all inwardly directed, toward Russians, whereas Hitler's crimes were outwardly directed, to the enemies outside. Hitler was more dangerous to Britain than Stalin, who was rather prudent in his foreign policy.

This is all true. But I believe that in addition to Churchill's political judgment, there was a moral judgment. This is how I understand his reference to "Hell" and "the Devil" in his reply to his secretary. He invoked hell and the devil because he believed he had to make a moral choice, not just a political choice. However, my task is to assess not Churchill's sincerity but the soundness of his moral judgment.

Churchill made this judgment well into the war. But one of the first Gallup polls was conducted in the United States in January 1939, before the Second World War broke out. Americans were asked a rather poignant question: if war should break out between the Soviet Union and Germany, whom would they prefer to win? The tally was 83 percent favoring a Soviet victory, as against 17 percent for Germany.[6] The Americans, like Churchill, were no friends of communism, and yet, in comparing the two, they clearly opted for Russia as the lesser evil. I believe that, naive and unworldly as those Americans were, they correctly sensed that in Hitler's racism there was something more sinister than in Stalin's frightfulness. There is no question that by the time the poll was conducted, millions of people had already been murdered under Stalin. The politically caused famine of 1932–1933 alone brought about the death of some six million people. But even if we compare the "purges" that Stalin launched in the Communist Party to Hitler's in the National Socialist Party, Hitler by then had very little to show in comparison to Stalin's liquidation of 700,000 people in the Great Purge of 1937–1938.

The Devil's Accountant

Some languages have a curious arithmetic. They count, "One, two, three," and then go on to "many"; above three, matters blur. Having been born in a relatively hot country, I believed that every temperature below zero Celsius is more or less the same—just very cold. Only after experiencing some cold winters abroad did I realize that –10C feels very different from –20C. When it comes to the numbers of people killed, we believe that above a certain threshold, it all blurs, that the number of the dead passes as "many." But morally, numbers should count. Murdering two million people is twice as bad as murdering one million.

This does not mean that sheer numbers affect what impression the killing makes on us. In a curious way, the converse is almost true. The Romans crucified thousands upon thousands, but only one crucifixion—and that one for only three days—made such a momentous impression on humanity. More was written of the death of Anne Frank than of the million and a half other Jewish children murdered in the Holocaust. Numbers register almost inversely to our ability to identify with the victims. Large numbers numb; individual stories make for vivid impressions. But moral arithmetic is not about impressions.

"A murder is a murder" is a deep tautology. Morally we should count all the murdered as equal. If so, to compare Stalin's regime to Hitler's regime, we just have to compare the number of people murdered by each. Of course, the two regimes committed other evil deeds, but these pale in comparison with mass murders. So let us stick to the numbers of the dead, if we agree that they were indeed murdered, not just killed.

On the principle that the life of each human counts as one, no less and no more, the cardinal evil of mass murder should be measured by cardinal numbers, and by cardinal numbers alone. Once murder has been determined, it is an additive function. In this view, we should not pay attention to other considerations and to other numbers; they all dim our moral judgment. We should not, for example, toy with ratios, such as the ratio of those murdered to the total population, or with counting children, or women, or the elderly. The relevant population is humanity at large and nothing else. Thus the ratio of the victims to the total population in Cambodia's Pol Pot massacre (one-fourth of the population), which is much higher than the ratio of the victims in Mao's China (about one-twelfth of the population), still does not place Pol Pot in Mao's league. Mao's regime was responsible for sixty-five million dead, as compared to a meager two million in Pol Pot's regime.[7]

In court (at least in some courts), a serial killer gets a string of life sentences according to the number of his or her victims. This is a symbolic token of the principle that murder is murder and each life counts the same, all on an individual basis. Any other principle of evaluating the degree of evil in mass murder above and beyond the number of people killed is wrong. Genocide in this view is not more evil, qua murder, than murdering a comparable number of people not identified by religion or ethnic affiliation. Murdering, say, the Budapest Quartet is not more evil qua murder than murdering four people taken at random. The genocide of the Jews, and with it the destruction of their culture, should not count as more evil than the murdering of kulaks just because kulaks belonged not to a cultural group but merely to a bureaucratic category, previously imposed from above by Stolypin (1906). Genocide usually inflicts further evil consequences that may be lacking in an anonymous mass murder, such as the destruction of valuable forms of life, or—in the case of the Budapest Quartet—a terrible loss to music. But these further evils should not be compounded with the evil of murder.

What makes genocide a horrendous crime, however, above and beyond horrific indiscriminate mass killing, is that genocide is a manifestation of dismembering the idea of shared humanity. By targeting a specific category of human beings as creatures that do not deserve to live, genocide removes this category from humankind.

Jonathan Glover is undoubtedly correct in writing, "The numbers of people murdered by Stalin's tyranny far surpass those killed in the Nazi camps."[8] But this comparison between the two is far from telling us the whole moral story. A great deal depends on who is responsible, in our opinion, for World War II victims in Europe. I put them on Hitler's account.

Does this mean that the 700,000 or so German civilians killed by the Allies' bombing of Germans cities should be added to Hitler's account? Is not Churchill himself accountable for killing those German civilians? Should Russian soldiers fighting on a battlefield be counted as people murdered?

The moral counting of the dead in the Second World War is indeed not a straightforward matter, as the example of the German civilians killed by the Allies shows. Moreover, it sounds to me quite absurd to regard all of the German soldiers, many of whom were great enthusiasts of the Nazi regime, as victims of that regime—as some German conservatives represent them today. Still, as tricky as billing the account of the deaths of World War II may be, and allowing for discounts in all doubtful cases, Hitler's hellish bill is such that it grossly surpasses that of Stalin in the years of terror.

To wit, the moral accountability for the dead is not a simple mechanical counting of corpses. The bodies of Red Army soldiers cannot be lumped with the bodies of Russian children. Soldiers can fight, and children cannot; hence the two cannot be lumped together as victims. Yet there is something proper in the mechanical criterion of measuring degree of evil by the number of victims. And my claim is that if we add to the responsibility of the Nazi regime all the victims of World War II, not just those who were murdered in the camps, Stalin's regime, hideous as it was, comes out as the lesser evil not in degree but in kind.

The Nature of the Victims

As a first approximation, Stalin's regime murdered its own people, whereas Hitler's regime murdered other people. One could be a loyal Nazi and feel secure in Hitler's Germany. No one except Stalin could ever feel secure under Stalin's rule. In fact, owing to Stalin's downright paranoia, even Stalin did not feel secure, as the affair of the Jewish doctors' plot indicates.

Stalin's reign of terror was random. A quota of victims had to be filled, regardless of any wrongdoing. Innocent people were routinely rounded up, many of them party loyalists. Indeed, Stalin's terror was directed toward party members as much as, if not more than, toward outsiders. This created the curious perception (one infused with a great deal of reality) that many of the perpetrators in Stalin's system were also its victims. So it was not as simple as what Akhmatova described as the two Russias, one sending the other to the camps. Stalin executed even heads of the NKVD like Yezhov and Yagoda, who had been his relentless executioners in the worst of times in the thirties. They, too, beside Bukharin, Rykov, Kresinsky, and for that matter Trotsky, fell under the ambiguous category of perpetrators-victims.

There was nothing like this in Nazi Germany. Apart from the Rohm purge, Hitler did very little to harm party loyalists or any other kind of loyalists. The Gestapo terror was directed toward political rivals such as the communists, or toward minorities such as the Jews.

Hitler's rule was largely a prime-mover's rule, the rule of an unmoved mover. Aristotle's example of an unmoved mover is of a loved one unaware of being loved and who nonetheless causes others to act and to try hard to second-guess her wishes in order to fulfill them. What took place in Nazi Germany was not always an outcome of Hitler's explicit instructions. Nor was it a function of an impersonal political structure.

It was Hitler's role as the prime mover, who was sometimes an unmoved mover, that made the Nazi system work.[9]

The point, however, is that Hitler's rule over the Germans, except for a short period during his ascendancy to power, was not chiefly based on terror. The emphasis here, of course, is on the rule over the Germans, not over the nations he conquered during the war. In the conquered countries he reigned by terror and nothing but terror. Stalin's internal rule, by contrast, was based on terror as a crucial element, either because this was the only way to make his cruel command economy work, because there was no other way to move an immovable bureaucracy, because of his "despotic Asiatic" tendencies, or because of all these factors together.

Stalin's terror was not just rule by fear. It also served as a source of legitimacy in the eyes of the party members and sympathizers. Many of them believed they were not the only ones terrified of him, but that the enemies of the revolution were too. They wanted the enemies of the revolution to be scared. The loyalists believed that his brutality was a justified means of defending the revolution. It was the old idea of Ivan the Terrible, that fear and trembling are the sources of legitimacy and not just substitutes for it.

The triumphant Stalin, especially after World War II, like Ivan the Terrible after the victory over the Tartars and the Teutonic Knights, ruled not just by fear and trembling but also by fear and admiration. But what does this account, if true, have to do with our moral comparison between the two regimes?

For one thing, it calls for a distinction between comparing Stalin and Hitler, on the one hand, and comparing the regimes of Stalin and of Hitler, on the other. We tend to conflate the two and to refer to the regimes by the synecdoche "Hitler" or "Stalin," much as we refer to the two individuals. But even if we maintain that the individuals Hitler and Stalin were equally evil, or that Stalin was even more wicked than Hitler, the regimes in terms of the people involved should be assessed differently. In one regime its own people were terrorized, and this is partly why they committed their evil deeds. In the other regime, they did it willingly. Hitler's people did what they did willingly, whereas many of Stalin's people were coerced into evil by a stupefying fear. One should not buy Khrushchev's interpretation, delineated in his famous secret speech to the Twentieth Party Conference, which claimed that Stalin and Stalin alone was responsible for the terror, while the rest were all his victims. Or, as he expressed it, "But as I later told Mikoyan, 'When Stalin says dance, a wise man dances.'"[10] Many, not Stalin alone, created the monstrous rule of terror, and Khrushchev himself had a great deal to do with it. And yet there is something right about his account. It is the ambiguity of the *victim-perpetrator* relationship that makes the case of Stalinism more morally ambiguous than the univocal case of Hitlerism.

The Moral Status of Fellow Travelers

The moral comparison between Stalinism and Hitlerism involves the moral comparison between the sympathizers of the two regimes. What excuses those who lived under a regime of terror does not excuse those sympathizers not subjected to Stalinist terror. The Soviet population supported Stalin's regime vociferously. So what makes Drieu La Rochelle, a Nazi sympathizer of his own will, moral anathema, and why do we have a soft spot for Louis Aragon, the Stalinist enthusiast? After all, it was Aragon who wrote the despicable poem "Prelude to the Cherry Season" (1931) with its recurrent mantra "Long live the GPU." There is no question that we would have treated him very differently had he written, "Long live the Gestapo." But in fact the GPU, better known by its later acronym of NKVD, was an instrument of oppression far more ubiquitous than the Gestapo. Until the war, there were about 8,000 Gestapo torturers, as compared to 350,000 in the GPU.

It is this kind of question about the moral equivalence of, say, Aragon and La Rochelle that gives rise to the feeling that the moral comparison between Hitlerism and Stalinism deals simply with settling scores with former communists and their fellow travelers. But exposing the hypocrisy of the pro-Soviet Left is not enough of a serious moral question to test our moral theories against. Those who raise the issue of the lesser evil between communism and Nazism may well have such a motive. Still, this does not mean that we should not be troubled by the question why there are former Stalinists among our best friends, but not former Hitlerists, and why we make allowances for them that we would never dare make for Hitlerists. "Speak for yourself," you may retort. But I don't think that I am speaking only for myself in raising this semiautobiographical question.

No question that in the 1930s some people sensed there was something wrong with Stalin's Russia, but believed that they were facing in an acute form the question of the lesser evil. The only force, they reasoned, both able to stop Nazism and committed to doing so was Communism. Given that the real moral choice was between Communism and Nazism, they opted for Communism on the lesser-evil argument.[11] What made it easier to pose the problem in such terms were agitprop agents with a real flair for propaganda, like Willi Munzenberg. Such skillful propagandists were clever enough to change the vocabulary of the choice by creating "popular fronts" that posed the question as a choice between Fascism and Anti-Fascism. Siding with Russia was simply the only efficient way of combating Fascism. After the war many of those who made such a choice of the lesser evil in the thirties were grateful for the heroism of the Red Army and for the Russian people's sacrifices in the war that brought Hitler down. They remained loyal to Russia and its wartime leader as an act of gratitude. These sympathizers had to cope with the embarrassing episode of the pact between Hitler and Stalin, but the heroism of Stalingrad later on more than made up for it.

Of course, not all Stalin's sympathizers were of the lesser-evil type; most were communists who viewed his communism as a positive good rather than a lesser evil. And many of those who had embraced communism were morally motivated, whereas no one embraced Nazism for moral reasons. This is significant. Communism offered a moral vision; Nazism did not. And many were attracted to the moral vision of a nonexploitative classless society. But I would like to address a different kind of supporters, those clearheaded enough to see that there was something deeply disturbing about Stalinism, and yet convinced that Stalinism was the lesser evil. Were these people justified?

In asking this question I do not ask whether they were right in believing that the situation was one of a simple choice between Communism and Nazism. But rather, since that is what they believed, were they allowed to side morally with Stalin at the time? Well, they were entitled, as Churchill was, to believe in the lesser-evil argument. True, Churchill also believed that the choice was not either Communism or Fascism but a much better third alternative: *he himself.* In the appeasement atmosphere of the time it is hard to blame those who believed in the either-Fascism-or-Communism view of the world.

I claim therefore not that those popular front people can be forgiven for their factual assessment of the world, but rather that they were very much entitled to their moral assessment of the lesser evil, just as Churchill was right in preferring the devil to Hitler. I still believe, however, that they were all wrong at the time in their lesser-evil argument, since, judging by conventional standards of decency and justice, Stalin's regime in the thirties was by no means the lesser evil of the two. And yet these people sensed something right and important, namely, that Hitler introduced an altogether new and different kind of evil.

Attack on Morality Itself

An important distinction between Communism and Nazism is that Nazism is an attack on the very idea of morality, whereas Communism, perverse as it was under Stalinism, does not attack morality as such. The idea is that the main premise of morality is shared humanity. Nazi racism, both in doctrine and in practice, was a conscious attack on the idea of shared humanity, and hence on the very possibility of morality itself. Stalinism was a terrible doctrine, not just in practice, but it did not amount to the very denial of shared humanity. Or so I shall argue.

Though I borrow from Kant the expression "radical evil," I do not borrow its content. In my use *radical evil* is any attack on morality itself. By attack I do not mean just a doctrinal nihilistic assault on the idea of morality but an assault through a combination of doctrine and practice. Nazism, in this sense, is radically evil.

Stuart Hampshire, too, regards Nazism as an attack on morality and not just as a gross violation of morality. But Hampshire emphasizes Nazism's attack on the idea of justice. Understanding justice as the constraints we humans impose on two human urges—toward domination and toward amassing a greater share of the rewards for ourselves—then Nazism, in Hampshire's view, is all about unrestricted domination.

I emphasize what I regard as the chief premise of morality, namely, the idea that all human beings should be subjected to moral treatment solely because they are human. Setting aside "soft" racism, in the sense of trivial racial prejudices, the hard racism of the Nazi variety—that which calls for eradicating "inferior" races such as the Jews and the Gypsies and for subjugating the Slavs—is a flagrant negation of the idea of shared humanity. Acting on such negation of shared humanity, as the Nazi regime clearly did, is promoting radical evil. It undermines morality itself.

A rotten compromise is rotten because it undermines morality. Hitler was not unique in undermining morality. But the distinction I am drawing here is between undermining morality in *deeds* and undermining morality in *deeds and in doctrine*—exactly what Hitlerism did.

Let us distinguish between *external* evil and *internal* evil. External evil is radical evil that amounts to a denial of the moral point of view in deed and doctrine. Internal evil comprises a gross undermining of morality in deed without denying moral points of view in doctrine. In terms of this distinction, the question is, should we exempt Stalinism from the charge of radical evil?

Was Stalinism Radically Evil?

Does Marxism undermine morality in doctrine? Did Stalin undermine morality not only in *deed* but also in *doctrine*? The first question is tricky. Marxism's is an ambivalent doctrine of morality. It is motivated by the moral idea of the evil of exploitation and dehumanization due to alienation.

Moreover, Marxism has an attitude to morality that I strongly support in this book: "a society is not the temple of value-idols that figure on the front of its monuments or in its constitutional scrolls; the value of a society is the value it places upon man's relation to man."[12]

Yet it views morality as an ideology, as a set of values and ideals that emerge in particular historical circumstances and function to consolidate the economic and social order of that historical stage. Moreover, morality was perceived by orthodox Marxism as a sentimental ideology, masking class conflict with abstract ("bourgeois") talk about humanity—which meant that bourgeois class interests pretended to be the universal interests of humanity. Revolutionary Marxists boasted of their toughness and uncompromising commitment to the class war: any appeal beyond class to shared humanity was suspicious.

Stalin was molded as a hardened revolutionary Marxist, to the point that class for him played almost the role that race played for social Darwinists. For social Darwinists, war among races is a biological necessity obeying the laws of biology. For hardened Marxists, unyielding class war is a historical necessity obeying the laws of history. So no real difference emerges between the two views with regard to shared humanity. Moreover, Stalin and Stalinists treated class origin as destiny. All those brought up in a bourgeois family, in their view, retained indelible bourgeois tendencies throughout their lives; no matter how loyal they were to the cause, they remained suspect. Class origin could be invoked as an indictment at any time—as occurred during the purges of the 1930s. All these statements are very true and very real, especially relating to Stalin's personal attitude to morality.

Yet the sway of Marxism on Stalinism still retained in doctrine, though not in practice, Marx's moral aspiration. By Stalinism, I mean an extenuated form of Leninism and not a separate new ideology. Creating a classless society for all humanity in which there would be no exploitation was more than the official line of the party for propaganda purposes. It was a deeply held doctrine, and even if shrouded in "dialectical" talk rather than in a moral imperative, its moral force was recognized by many and was a source of attraction for many, especially in the West.

Richard Overy, who commented astutely on the role of necessity, biological and historical, in the attitude of both toward morality, goes on quickly to mention their similarly hostile attitude toward Christianity, perhaps because they believed that morality is Christian morality.[13] But then there are Christians and Christians, much as there are Marxists and Marxists; in both cases, though, they are species of a common genus. One such Christian deserves our attention. Stalin's attitude toward morality even in its Marxist form does not differ materially from that of Tomás de Torquemada, the great Spanish inquisitor of the fifteenth century, toward Christ's moral teaching. One may very well ask whether Torquemada was a true Christian, much as one may ask whether Stalin was a true Marxist. My answer to both questions is a qualified yes. Both retained, albeit perversely, the idea of shared humanity. Hitler, however, did not retain the idea of shared humanity— though he kept using the term—not even perversely.

The question about Torquemada is same as the question that Ivan Karamazov asks about the Grand Inquisitor.[14] The Grand Inquisitor believes that by giving humanity a moral choice in the way Jesus understands it, he (Jesus) withholds redemption from most men and makes redemption the business of the few. By contrast, the Inquisitor believes that his actions aim at saving all men, and he does all he can to remove the burden of choice from humanity. Dostoevsky was torn by the issue of whether the Grand Inquisitor is an authentic Christian or whether he follows the Devil (as Ivan

Karamazov thought). Dostoevsky did not settle the question. But one thing is clear: Dostoevsky's Grand Inquisitor cares about humanity as a whole. The Grand Inquisitor differs from Christ in his assessment of human nature, but he cares about the salvation of humanity at large.

Marxist-Leninists in the Soviet Union under Stalin retained the moral vision of a nonexploitative classless society for humanity at large; this is a very different doctrine from Nazism, which rejected any form of recognized morality by essentially dividing humanity into immutable races.

The Withering Away of Morality

The Marxist-Leninist doctrine of class war destroying the state, seen as a bourgeois organ of repression, is well documented. But another doctrine related to the destruction of the state may be termed the withering away of morality. What is this (tacit) doctrine, and does it undermine morality?

In this Marxist view, both bourgeois economics and bourgeois morality are based on a common "naturalistic" assumption of scarcity: we humans face, in all societies and under all circumstances, competing demands on scarce resources. The well-known paradox of diamonds highlights this assumption. Why is the price of diamonds so much higher than the price of water, even though we need water to sustain our life and we can easily do without diamonds? The answer, according to Adam Smith, is scarcity. Compared to scarce diamonds, water is abundant, which is why water is cheaper than diamonds.

I have already mentioned that Aristotelian thinkers such as Maimonides thought that scarcity was a fact of the world of matter, but not of the world of the spirit. Hence the right way to live is the contemplative life of the spirit. This is precisely the tendency that Marxian thinking tries to block. Contemplative life is not the only form of life worth living, not even the preferred one. Moreover, it is not the only way to escape scarcity. If paradise is the dream of humanity, a life without scarcity, the Marxists believe there is no need for such wishful thinking. Properly understood, scarcity is a result of historical conditions, not of natural conditions. Scarcity can be overcome in historical times. It can be overcome, on the one hand, by technological innovations that will increase immeasurably what the material world can offer us. On the other hand, it can be overcome by the creation of a classless society with no competing claims on the available resources, with a different set of desires that will fulfill human true needs rather than desires shaped by an irrational urge for domination. The effect will be a radical change in human patterns of consumption, such that scarcity will no longer have dominion over human beings.

With scarcity gone, not only is economics gone, but morality withers away. In a world without scarcity, there is no need for morality any more than there was any need for Adam and Eve in paradise to eat from the tree of knowledge to know good from evil. Abundance undermines the need for a distinction between good and evil.

The question is whether this vision of overcoming scarcity, and hence undercutting morality, falls under the heading of undermining morality. My answer is, not in the least. The mere fact that Communism aspires to overcome morality by creating conditions such that it will no longer be needed, does not undermine morality any more than the aspiration to create a situation of perfect health undermines medicine.

Stalinism is morally a huge experiment in Pascal's wager.[15] A socialist world without any scarcity in the future has an infinite utility. The overwhelming expected utility of the future world justifies, on utilitarian grounds, any amount of suffering today. The infinite future bliss dwarfs the suffering of today on the ground of expected utility. This Pascalian wager of betting on future history is a bad argument, since if you pump infinite utility into future socialism or into kingdom come, anything goes. Every state of affairs has a tiny probability of bringing about the blissful future: multiply it by the infinite utility of the future and you get an infinite expected utility justifying that particular state of affairs. In short, the Stalinist use of Pascal's wager can justify fascism as much as it justifies communism. It can justify everything, and hence it justifies nothing.

But with all this moral sophistry about the blissful future, there are, of course, questions about the road, whether or not it leads to the Promised Land. Or, to switch to a more familiar metaphor, the question is whether, in addition to breaking eggs, Stalinism can produce an omelet. Put literally, were the means taken by Stalinism instrumentally adequate to bringing about the desired end?

If the end is a world without scarcity, then the answer should be a resounding no. But if the end was to create an industrial society that could stand up to enemies such as Nazi Germany, then the answer is yes. Awful as these means were, the outcome of World War II shows that they were indeed adequate for that goal. But this gambit of shifting the goal, at least temporarily, from socialism to industrialization is, morally speaking, a red herring. It was used by Stalinist apologetics to justify Stalin's choice of the right way to overcome Nazism—as if Communism was born to combat Nazism, and as if there never existed a pact between Stalin and Hitler, a pact that Stalin was determined to keep. It is a case of shooting first and drawing the bull's-eye later.

In the Name of Future Humanity

The practice of Stalinism was hellish but its ideals were moral. With Hitlerism, both the practice and the ideals were fiendish. So much the worse, some might say, for Stalinism. On this account, it is much worse to act immorally in the name of moral ideals, just as it is worse to be a hypocrite and act immorally than to act immorally without being hypocritical about it. The Nazis at least did not pretend to behave morally.

I disagree. The cliché that hypocrisy is the homage paid by vice to virtue has, I believe, a profound meaning. Hypocrisy, irritating as it is, at least recognizes morality; and Communism, even in its wretched Stalinist form, is not nihilism. Nazism, unlike Communism in general and Stalinism in particular, is a denial of shared humanity. This is my claim. But is it true?

In a chapter entitled "The Attack on Humanity" Jonathan Glover rightly points out that Nazi practices carried dehumanization to relentless extremes. My point is that not only the practice but also the doctrine denied a shared humanity. But then one asks whether it is true that the Nazi ideology, confused and confusing as it was, denied the idea of shared humanity. After all, Glover uses as a motto for one of his chapters these words from Hitler: "Those who see in National Socialism nothing more than a political movement, know scarcely anything of it. It is more even than a religion: it is the will to create mankind anew."[16] One may cogently argue that this idea would not be alien to Stalin, nor to Mao. They all talked and acted in the name of a future humanity they were going to create; none of them was committed to a concrete shared humanity. So why does it matter whether you are excluded from future humanity for being a parasitic bourgeois, as in Stalinism, or for being a parasitic Jew, as in Nazism? After all, both categories of human beings, bourgeois and Jews, were perceived in equally inhuman terms— as "parasites."

The idea of humanity's future and the idea of shaping "a new man" are fantasies of many ideologies. Moreover, the idea that one class of people anticipates man's future and humanity's future, be they "the workers," "the bureaucrats," or "the students," is also an idea shared by many radical ideologies. With it goes the idea that the humanity of today is, in biblical terms, a "desert generation" that will perish on the way to the Promised Land. Stalinism, I maintain, is an extreme case of this dangerous fantasy of callousness toward the concrete people of today in the name of abstract future humanity.

But Hitlerism is something very different. It is the dismembering of humanity into races. It thereby excludes, as a matter of doctrine, groups of people from deserving moral consideration of any sort. If the Slavs are destined in Hitler's "future humanity" to be slaves, the ontological and moral status of the Slavs is no better than that of domestic animals.

When it comes to Nazism, there is no room for morality. At most we can find in Nazism a perverse hygiene, run by categories of filth. Filth is regarded as a degenerative disease, and thereby as the degeneration of the master race. Future humanity in Hitler's fantasy is not humanity: the master race replaces the idea of humanity. This is radical evil if anything is. So in my view, Churchill was right in preferring Stalin to Hitler, or in his language, the Devil to Herr Hitler, not because the former was a lesser evil in degree but because he was a lesser evil in kind.

NOTES

INTRODUCTION: WHY COMPROMISE?

1. Reported to me by Robert Schulman.

2. *The Day after Trinity: Robert Oppenheimer and the Atomic Bomb*, directed by Jon Else (1981).

3. Attributed to the poet George Herbert.

4. Joseph Conrad, *Heart of Darkness*, ed. D.C.R.A Goonetillke, 2nd ed. (Peterborough, Ont.: Broadview Press, 1999).

5. Neal Ascherson, *The King Incorporated: Leopold the Second and the Congo* (London: Granta Books 1999), 102.

6. Adam Hochschild, *King Leopold's Ghost: A Story of Greed, Terror, and Heroism in Colonial Africa* (London: Macmillan, 1998).

7. Avishai Margalit, "Ideals and Second Bests," in *Philosophy for Education*, ed. Seymour Fox (Jerusalem: Van Leer Foundation, 1983), 77–90.

8. R. Lipsey and K. Lancaster, "The General Theory of Second-Best," *Review of Economic Studies* 24, no. 1 (1956): 11–32.

9. W. B. Gallie, "Art as an Essentially Contested Concept," *Philosophical Quarterly* 6, no. 23 (April 1956): 97–114. W. B. Gallie, "Essentially Contested Concepts," *Proceedings of the Aristotelian Society* 56 (1956): 167–198.

10. Heinrich von Kleist, *Michael Kohlhaas* (1810) (New York: Melville House, 2005). Kleist's book is about a sixteenth-century law-abiding horse dealer, Kohlhaas, who has been wronged. In his mad pursuit of redress for the injustice done to him, he brings about horrific destruction.

11. *Heraclitus Fragments* in Greek (Unicode) and English, DK 80, at www.heraclitusfragments.com. See Stuart Hampshire, *Justice Is Conflict* (Princeton, N.J.: Princeton University Press, 2000).

12. Babylonian Talmud, tractate Yevamoth (65 b).

13. Babylonian Talmud, tractate Sanhedrin (64).

14. The controversy has to do with the nature of justice. Justice is of divine origin, and thus it is not up to human judges to deviate from the prescribed divine justice and pursue compromises that bypass justice, for the sake of something else. The opposite argument starts with the same premise: since

justice has a divine source, the judge is at a tremendous risk of getting it wrong. A mistake by the judge in administering divine justice is not a simple error but a sin. Thus it is better to try settling disputes in the mundane way of compromise than to risk a sinful miscarriage of divine justice.

15. This view might take the form of value monism: there is only one fundamental value, which is justice; all other values stand to it either as constitutive parts or as instrumentally contributive factors. In this view, no plurality of independent values can clash.

16. Quoted in Max H. Bazerman, "Why Negotiations Go Wrong," in *The Negotiation Sourcebook*, ed. Ira G. Asherman and Sandra Vance Asherman, 2nd ed. (Amherst, Mass.: HRD Press, 2001), 219.

CHAPTER 1: TWO PICTURES OF POLITICAL COMPROMISE

1. *Parliamentary Debates*, 5th ser., vol. 339 (1938), October 5, 1938.

2. A.J.P. Taylor claims that the terms of Munich were much closer to what Chamberlain proposed in Berchtesgaden than what Hitler offered at Bad Godesberg. See the discussion in Niall Ferguson, *The War of the World: Twentieth-Century Conflict and the Descent of the West* (New York: The Penguin Press, 2006), 361f.

3. Eric Maskin raised with me the following question: what was Hitler's concession in the Munich agreement that would render the agreement a "compromise"? It seems, he says, that Hitler made no concession; if so, then the Munich agreement does not amount to a compromise, and hence it does not serve as a paradigmatic case of a rotten compromise.

The issue is not whether Hitler made *in fact* a concession (he did not); the issue is whether Hitler made a *prima facie* concession. His promise to give up further demands in Europe, specifically, to give up on Germans' aspiration to redress in full "the injustice of Versailles" was indeed a prima facie concession.

Many people in Europe at the time did believe that the German grievances with regard to the Versailles agreement were justified. Most people in Britain held the belief that for Germany not to make further claims is a concession all right.

For more on making concessions relative to a "dream point," see chapter 2.

4. From http://doctor-horsefeathers.com/archives/2003.php.

5. French Constitution, Article 1, October 4, 1958.

6. R. Chang, ed., *Incommensurability, Incomparability, and Practical Reason* (Cambridge: Harvard University Press, 1997).

7. See http://en.wikiquote.org/wiki/Talk:F._Scott_Fitzgerald.

8. Oscar Wilde, *Lady Windermere's Fan*, in *The Importance of Being Earnest and Other Plays*, (London: Penguin, 1940), act 3.

9. Alan Fiske and Philip Tetlock, "Taboo Trade-offs: Reactions to Transactions That Transgress the Spheres of Justice," *Political Psychology* 18, no. 2 (1997): 255–297.

10. James Griffin, *Well-Being: Its Meaning, Measurement and Moral Importance* (Oxford: Oxford University Press 1989), 83.

11. William Shakespeare, *The Merchant of Venice*, ed. Jay L. Halio, Oxford World's Classics (Oxford: Oxford University Press, 1998), 1.3.153.

12. "Reparations Agreement between Israel and West Germany," at http://en.wikipedia.org/wiki/Reparations_Agreement_between_Israel_and_West_Germany.

13. The conventional account of the Bible as grudgingly accepting voluntary slavery is highly misleading. The Hebrew Bible in the book of Exodus does not describe anything like voluntary choice on the part of the one who remains when he can go free; it depicts coercion. It is not the love of the slave for his master that makes him want to stay enslaved; it is his love for his wife and children. "21:4 If his master have given him a wife, and she have born him sons or daughters; the wife and her children shall be her master's, and he shall go out by himself. 21:5 And if the servant shall plainly say, I love my master, my wife, and my children; I will not go out free." The slave saying that he loves his master and remains enslaved as his concession to stay with his family. Such a slave deserves our admiration, not our admonition; to pierce his ear with an awl is just adding insult to injury. The biblical slave who lends his ear to the awl does not make a rotten compromise but is engaged in an honorable defeat—sharing the burden with his family.

14. David Hume, *Enquiry concerning the Principles of Morals*, ed. L. A. Selby-Bigge, 3rd ed. rev. P. H. Nidditch (Oxford: Clarendon Press, 1975), bk. 3, sec. 2; *Dialogues concerning Natural Religion*, ed. Norman Kemp Smith (Oxford: Oxford University Press, 1935), pt. 10.

CHAPTER 2: VARIETIES OF COMPROMISE

1. See, however, John P. Conley, Rich McLean, and Simon Wilkie, "Axiomatic Foundations for Compromise Theory: The Duality of Bargaining

Theory and Multi-Objective Programming," at http://www.vanderbilt
.edu/Econ/jpconley/documents/COOP-games/dual-bargain.pdf; Young-
sub Chun and William Thomson, "Bargaining Problems with Claims,"
Mathematical Social Sciences 24, no. 1 (August 1992): 19–33.

2. Abhinay Muthoo, *Bargaining Theory with Application* (Cambridge:
Cambridge University Press, 1999).

3. George Lowenstein, Leigh Thompson, and Max Bazerman, "Social
Utility and Decision Making in Interpersonal Context," *Journal of Person-
ality and Social Psychology* 57, no. 3 (1989): 426–441.

4. I leave the expression "form of recognition" vague, indeed as a placeholder to be filled by, among other things, expressions such as "political
recognition," "legal recognition," "moral recognition," or even "recognition
of the humanity of the other."

5. However, my sense of "dream point" is exogenous to the game: "a
dream" is more a wishful payoff than an expected payoff, which is the "aspiration point" in the game theory lingo.

6. Indeed, for a while, it looked like a major compromise and a major
achievement: Israel recognizing the PLO and the PLO recognizing Israel's
right to exist. This has changed, unfortunately, with the Hamas government and Israel refusing to recognize each other.

7. Thomas C. Schelling, "An Essay on Bargaining," *American Economic
Review* 46, no. 3 (June 1956): 282.

8. Richard Thaler, "Towards a Positive Theory of Consumer Choice,"
Journal of Economic Behavior and Organization 1 (1980): 39–60.

9. See James Fearon, "Rationalist Explanations for War," *International
Organization* 49, no. 3 (1995): 379–414.

10. I owe this point to Menachem Yaari.

11. Statement to the Knesset by President Sadat, November 20, 1977:

To speak frankly, our land does not yield itself to bargaining. It is
not even open to argument. To us, the national soil is equal to the
holy valley where God Almighty spoke to Moses—peace be upon
him. None of us can, or accept to, cede one inch of it, or accept the
principle of debating or bargaining over it.

Israel Ministry of Foreign Affairs, vols. 4–5 (1977–1979), at http://www
.mfa.gov.il/mfa/foreign relations/israels Foreign Relations since 1947/1977-
1979/73 Statement to the Knesset by President Sadat-20.

12. Robert Nozick, "Coercion," in *Philosophy, Science and Method: Essays in Honor of Ernest Nagel*, ed. Sidney Morgenbesser, Patrick Suppes, and Morton White (New York: St. Martin's, 1969). Alan Wertheimer, *Coercion: Studies in Moral, Political, and Legal Philosophy* (Princeton, N.J.: Princeton University Press, 1987).

13. Robert Dahl, *How Democratic Is the American Constitution?*, 2nd ed. (New Haven, Conn.: Yale University Press, 2003), 15–16.

14. William Lloyd Garrison, "Abolitionist William Lloyd Garrison Admits of No Compromise with the Evil of Slavery" (1854), in *Lend Me Your Ears: Great Speeches in History*, ed. William Safire (New York: W. W. Norton, 1992).

15. William Lloyd Garrison, "To the Public," *The Liberator*, January 1, 1831.

16. William Lloyd Garrison, "Resolution adopted by the Massachusetts Anti-Slavery Society" (January 27, 1843). Cited in Walter M. Merrill, *Against Wind and Tide: A Biography of William Lloyd Garrison* (Cambridge: Harvard University Press, 1963), 205.

17. Ibid., n. 5.

18. Compare Paul Finkelman, *Slavery and the Founders: Race and Liberty in the Age of Jefferson* (London: M. E. Sharpe, 2001); Evan Carton, *Patriotic Treason: John Brown and the Soul of America* (London: Free Press, 2006).

19. Adam Smith, *The Wealth of Nations*, introd. Jonathan B. Wright (Hampshire: Harriman House, 2007), 53, 252.

20. James Madison, *Notes of Debates in the Federal Convention of 1787, Reported by James Madison*, Bicentennial ed. (New York: W. W. Norton, 1987), 530.

21. Rome statute of the International Criminal Court (http://www.preventgenocide.org/law/icc/statute/part-a.htm#2), Article 7: Crimes against humanity. For discussion see Larry May, *Crimes against Humanity: A Normative Account* (Cambridge: Cambridge University Press, 2005).

Chapter 3: Compromising for Peace

1. Immanuel Kant, "Toward Lasting Peace: A Philosophical Sketch" (1795), in *Kant's Political Writings*, ed. Hans Reiss (Cambridge: Cambridge University Press, 1991), 93.

2. Robert Nozick, *Anarchy, State, and Utopia* (New York: Basic Books, 1974), 149–182.

3. http://www.quotationspage.com/quotes/J. What Getty actually said was "The meek shall inherit the Earth, but not its mineral rights."

4. Moshe Halbertal and Avishai Margalit, *Idolatry* (Cambridge: Harvard University Press, 1992).

5. In his autobiography Leon Trotsky writes that on January 11, 1919, he sent a telegram to Lenin in which he said, "Compromise is of course necessary, but not one that is rotten" (*My Life: An Attempt at an Autobiography* [New York: C. Scribner's Sons, 1930], chap. 36). Four years later, Trotsky writes, "Lenin returned to the phrase almost word for word" when writing to him that "Stalin will make a rotten compromise and then he will deceive us." This may very well be the origin of the expression "rotten compromise."

6. Muhammed Ibn Ismaiel Al-Bukhari, *Shih al-Bukhari* 3.891. English translation by Muhammad Muhsin Khan, at http://www.usc.edu/schools/college/crcc/engagement/resources/texts/muslim/hadith/bukhari/.

7. Frances Kamm, "Making War (and Its Continuation) Unjust," *European Journal of Philosophy* 9, no. 3 (2001): 328–343.

8. John Maynard Keynes, *The Economic Consequences of the Peace* (New York: Skyhorse Publishing, 2007), 14.

9. A peace brought about by the total destruction of the enemy, as Carthage was destroyed by the Romans in the Third Punic War.

CHAPTER 4: COMPROMISE AND POLITICAL NECESSITY

1. I owe this example to Mahmood Mamdani.

2. Niall Ferguson, *The War of the World: Twentieth-Century Conflict and the Descent of the West* (New York: The Penguin Press, 2006), 587.

3. In my sense, tragic choices does not denote the tragic choices of allocating tragically scarce resources, as in Guido Calabresi and Philip Bobbitt, *Tragic Choices* (New York:W. W. Norton, 1978).

4. I owe this example to Paul Rozin.

5. http://net.lib.byu.edu/~rdh7/wwi/versailles.html.

6. I owe this sentence to David Hallway.

7. Julius Epstein, *Operation Keelhaul: The Story of Forced Repatriation from 1944 to the Present* (Old Greenwich, Conn.: Devin Adair, 1973), 1.

8. Nicholas Bethell, *The Last Secret: Forcible Repatriation to Russia 1944–7,* introd. Hugh Trevor-Roper (London: Andre Deutsch, 1974).

9. Nikolai Tolstoy, *The Secret Betrayal 1944–1947* (New York, Charles Scribner's Sons, 1977), 20–21.

10. Alexander Solzhenitsyn, *The Gulag Archipelago 1918–1956*, trans. Thomas P. Whitney and Harry Willetts (New York: HarperCollins, 2002), pt. 1, chap. 6.

11. See Bethell, *The Last Secret*, ix.

12. See Tolstoy, *The Secret Betrayal*, 413.

13. Ibid., 422.

14. Bethell, *The Last Secret*, 8.

15. Ibid., 11.

16. Ibid., 10.

17. I thank Jonathan Greenberg for drawing my attention to the notion of "aid and abet" in the law.

18. Leszek Kolakowski, *My Correct Views on Everything* (South Bend, Ind.: St. Augustine's Press, 2005), 9.

19. In private conversation.

20. Martin Gilbert, *Winston S. Churchill*, vol. 7, *Road to Victory, 1941–1945* (Boston: Houghton Mifflin 1986), 1232.

21. Evan Esar, *20,000 Quips & Quotes* (New York: Barnes and Noble Publishers, 1968), 857.

22. Ashton Applewhite, William R. Evans III, and Andrew Frothingham, *And I Quote—* (New York: St. Martin's Press, 1992), 48.

23. Maimonides, *The Laws of the Basic Principles of the Torah*, chap. 5, sec. 4.

24. Reinhold Niebuhr, *Moral Man and Immoral Society: A Study in Ethics and Politics* (1932; Louisville, Ky.: Westminster John Knox Press, 2001).

25. Bertrand Russell, *Mysticism and Logic* (1917; Mineola, N.Y.: Dover Publications, 2004), 47.

Chapter 5: The Morality of Rotten Compromises

1. Avishai Margalit, *The Ethics of Memory* (Cambridge: Harvard University Press, 2002).

2. I do not consider relations to be ethical unless they pass a threshold of morality. But here for the sake of contrast I ignore this requirement.

3. Benedict Anderson, *Imagined Communities: Reflections on the Origin and Spread of Nationalism*, rev. ed. (London: Verso, 1991).

4. Not all thick relations yield ethical relations. Blood feuds can erupt between very thick blood relations.

5. The tribal picture differs from Hobbes's picture of man as wolf in assuming not individual egotism but only collective egotism. A tribal picture of social relations has room for the stranger who happens to be a guest: he is the object of the tribe's generosity and commitment to protect him as a guest. The wickedness of Sodom or Gibeah (Judges 19) is the inhospitality to the stranger, whereas Abraham is the biblical embodiment of the gracious host. But this generous attitude to strangers with whom one has only distant relations is a temporary extension of ethical relations with strangers who, in the language of Lot, "come under the shadow of my roof." The stranger under one's roof, not the stranger in general, has this special status.

6. John Locke, *The Works*, vol. 2 (Aalen, Germany: Scientia Verlag, 1963), 224–225.

7. Carl Schmitt, *Political Theology: Four Chapters on the Concept of Sovereignty*, trans. George D. Schwab (1922; Cambridge: MIT Press, 1985); University of Chicago edition, with an introduction by Tracy B. Strong (Chicago: University of Chicago Press, 2004). Carl Schmitt, *The Concept of the Political*, trans. George D. Schwab (1927; Chicago: University of Chicago Press, 1996; exp. ed., with an introduction by Tracy B. Strong, 2006). Giorgio Agamben, *State of Exception*, trans. Kevin Attell (Chicago: University of Chicago Press, 2005).

8. Avishai Margalit, "Open Texture," in *Meaning and Use*, ed. Avishai Margalit (Dordrecht: D. Reidel, 1979), 141–152.

9. *Life*, December 5, 1960, 146.

10. Judgment of Judge Benjamin Halevi, Criminal Case 124/53; *Attorney General v. Malchiel Greenwald*, District Court, Jerusalem, June 22, 1955, http://www.fantompowa.net/Flame/judge_halevi.htm.

11. Thomas Hobbes, *Leviathan* (1651), pt. 1, chap. 13.

12. Indeed, Richelieu became an emblem of the principle of raison d'état, according to which the interest of the state is the sole consideration of a statesman and the only source of legitimacy. In spite of his being a cleric, it is he who is perceived as having asserted the autonomy of politics, freed from confessional considerations.

This, however, is not the view Richelieu had on his own politics. He maintained that in dealing with Protestants (Sweden, the Netherlands, and some Protestant German principalities) as against Catholics (Spain and Austria) he was acting according to the dictates of natural law, especially according to the necessity of self-defense, as well as the requirement of protecting the needy.

His self-serving account may be taken as another sign of his cynicism; however, J. H. Eliot makes a strong case for the sincerity of Richelieu's view of himself. I am willing to believe that Richelieu was sincere. But then he was wrong rather than dishonest.

Making Richelieu an emblem of raison d'état is not, in my view, a mistake.

See J. H. Eliot, *Richelieu and Olivares* (Cambridge: Cambridge University Press, 1991), chap. 5.

13. Compare Hans Morgenthau, *Politics among Nations: The Struggle for Power and Peace* (1948; New York: Knopf, 1973).

14. Jean-Paul Sartre, "Existentialism Is a Humanism," trans. Philip Mairet, in *Existentialism from Dostoevsky to Sartre*, ed. Walter Kaufmann (New York: Meridian, 1956), 287–311.

15. Mitchell N. Berman, "Justification and Excuse, Law and Morality," *Duke Law Journal* 53 (2003): col. 53, no. 1. J. C. Smith, "Justification and Excuse in the Criminal Law," *Modern Law Review* 52, no. 6 (1989): 868–869. Peter Westen and James Mangiafico, "The Criminal Defense of Duress: A Justification, Not an Excuse—And Why It Matters," *Buffalo Criminal Law Review* 6 (2003): 833.

Chapter 6: Sectarianism and Compromise

1. J. J. Saunders, *A History of Medieval Islam* (London: Routledge, 1990).

2. Maureen A. Tilley, *The Bible in Christian North Africa: The Donatist World* (Minneapolis: Fortress Press, 1997).

3. Norman Chon, *Noah's Flood: The Genesis Story in Western Thought* (New Haven: Yale University Press, 1996), 28–31.

4. Michael White, *De Stijl and Dutch Modernism* (Manchester: Manchester University Press, 2003).

5. Seymour Martin Lipset, *Continental Divide: The Values and Institutions of the United States and Canada* (New York: Routledge, 1990), 42–57.

6. Edna Ullmann-Margalit, *Out of the Cave: A Philosophical Inquiry into the Dead Sea Scrolls Research* (Cambridge: Harvard University Press, 2002), chap. 3.

7. In a lecture at Princeton University, winter 2007.

8. *The Encyclopedia of Islam*, new ed. (Leiden: E. J. Brill, 1965), 2:930–931. Michael Cook, *Early Muslim Dogma: A Source-Critical Study* (Cambridge: Cambridge University Press, 1981).

9. Johann Jakob Herzog, Philip Schaff, and Albert Hauck, eds., *Schaff-Herzog Encyclopedia of Religious Knowledge* (New York: Funk and Wagnalls, 1908–1914), 24–25. Jonathan D. Spence, *The Memory Palace of Matteo Ricci* (New York: Penguin, 1994).

10. Moshe Halbertal, *Concealment and Revelation: Esotericism in Jewish Thought and Its Philosophical Implications*, trans. Jackie Feldman (Princeton, N.J.: Princeton University Press, 2007), esp. 166–167.

11. See Gadi Yatziv, *The Sectorial Society* (Jerusalem: The Bialik Institue, 1999) (in Hebrew).

12. Alan Cameron, *Circus Factions: Blues and Greens at Rome and Byzantium* (Oxford: Clarendon Press, 1976).

13. Khaled Haroub, *Hamas: Political Thought and Practice* (Washington, D.C.: Institute for Palestinian Studies, 2000); Shaul Mishal and Avraham Sela, *The Palestinian Hamas: Vision, Violence, and Coexistence* (New York: Columbia University Press, 2000).

14. See James D. Fearon and David Laitin, "Ethnicity, Insurgency, and Civil War," *American Political Science Review* 97, no. 1 (2003): 57–90.

15. Jonathan J. Price, *Thucydides and Internal War* (Cambridge: Cambridge University Press, 2001).

16. *The Encyclopedia of Islam,* new ed., vol. 10 (2000), 134–135.

17. Gilles Kepel, *Fitna. Guerre au cœur de l'islam* (Paris: Gallimard, 2004).

18. Adam Przeworski, *Capitalism and Social Democracy* (Cambridge: Cambridge University Press, 1985).

CONCLUSION: BETWEEN EVIL AND RADICAL EVIL

1. Stuart Hampshire, *Innocence and Experience* (London: Jonathan Cape, 1999).

2. Gilbert Ryle, "Jane Austen and the Moralists," in *Collected Papers: Critical Essays and Collected Essays 1929–68*, vol. 1 (New York: Barnes and Noble, 1971).

3. Winston S. Churchill, *The Second World War*, vol. 3, *The Grand Alliance* (Boston: Mariner Books, 1986), 332.

4. Ibid., 379.

5. Churchill, *The Second World War*, 3:332–332.

6. Eric Hobsbaum, *The Age of Extremes: The Short Twentieth Century, 1914–1991* (London: Michael Joseph, 1994), 14.

7. Stéphane Courtois et al., *The Black Book of Communism*, trans. Jonathan Murphy and Mark Kramer (Cambridge: Harvard University Press, 1999).

8. Jonathan Glover, *Humanity: A Moral History of the Twentieth Century* (London: Jonathan Cape, 1999), 317.

9. Compare Ian Kershaw, *Hitler, 1936–1945: Nemesis* (New York: W. W. Norton, 2001); Ian Kershaw and Moshe Lewin, *Stalinism and Nazism: Dictatorships in Comparison* (Cambridge: Cambridge University Press, 1997).

10. "Khrushchev: Notes from a Forbidden Land," *Time*, November 30, 1970.

11. The best account is to be found in François Furet, *The Passing of an Illusion: The Idea of Communism in the Twentieth Century*, trans. Deborah Furet (Chicago: University of Chicago Press, 1999).

12. Maurice Merleau-Ponty, *Humanism and Terror*, trans. John O'Neill (Boston: Beacon Press, 1969), xiv.

13. Richard Overy, *The Dictators: Hitler's Germany and Stalin's Russia* (New York: W. W. Norton, 2004), chap. 7, "The Moral Universe of Dictatorship."

14. Fyodor Dostoevsky, *The Brothers Karamazov*, trans. Constance Garnett (New York: Barnes & Noble Classics, 2004), bk. 5, chap. 5.

15. BlaisePascal, *Pascal's Pensées,* trans. W. F. Trotter (New York: P. F. Collier and Son, 1910), 233.

16. Glover, *Humanity*, 315.

INDEX

211